BUILD
YOUR
PEOPLE

not your church

DO YOUR PART,
LET JESUS DO HIS

ALI ROOHI

Table of Contents

00   **FORWARD**

00   **INTRODUCTION**

00   **CHAPTER 1**
The Problem with Your Church

00   **CHAPTER 2**
You're Full of It!

00   **CHAPTER**
Break Up or Break Down

00   **CHAPTER**
The Hardest Person to Lead

00   **CHAPTER**
Define Who a Leader Is

00   **CHAPTER 6**
Curate Your Culture

00   **CHAPTER 7**
Say It, Don't Spray It

00   **CHAPTER 8**
See Others as God Does

00   **CHAPTER 9:**
Pick Your Team Wisely

00   **CHAPTER 10:**
Brush off Your Shoulder

00   **CHAPTER 11:**
How to Train Your Team

00   **CHAPTER 12:**
Delegate to Build

00   **CHAPTER 13:**
How to Correct Your Team

00   **CHAPTER 14:**
Inspire Your Team

102   **APPENDIX**

Introduction

THE LEADERSHIP CRISIS PROBLEM

It's a problem that pastors are keenly aware of: local churches never have enough leaders! Most churches claim to develop them and build them in house, but in reality most hire them. And let's face it, no church has enough money to solve all its problems with money.

So what do you do when you can't afford to add more people to your staff? What do you do when the needs in your church and community can't be solved with money? This is the crisis the church faces in America. The need is greater than the available resources.

THE BIGGER PROBLEM IN SILICON VALLEY

The problem is only intensified in Silicon Valley because:

1. There is no seminary in the Bay Area.
2. It has the highest cost of living in the U.S.
3. It is the most unchurched region in America.

Silicon Valley is filled with the wealthiest, stingiest, most pagan people in all of America. They want Mr. Benjamin, not Mr. Jesus.

Whatever problem the capital C church faces in America with declining church attendance, engagement and growth issues are only magnified in Silicon Valley.

WHAT'S THE SOLUTION?

If you can't **buy** leaders, you must **build** them. This book is not about information systems or leadership trips and tricks, but about changing your mindset. For example, we'll unpack what Tommy Barnett says: "Everything you need to reach your city is already in the house!" If you believe that statement, it will change your philosophy of ministry. It will give you a vision for building and developing the people you already have—and help you avoid simply wishing and day dreaming about those you don't.

WHY IS THIS BOOK IMPORTANT?

It's important to always start with the **WHY** before the **WHAT**. Why does the local church need leaders—and more of them? The "Why?" question get to the heart and motivation of this book, which is that God has given our church a very clear vision.

The vision of CenterSet church is to guide people into a growing relationship with Jesus!

This is why we exist as a church. We are about leading the lost and broken home at all costs. We are about helping and guiding everyone in Silicon Valley into a relationship with Jesus! Our heart is for all people, because all people are loved by Jesus. We make no apologies for being specifically focused on reaching the lost.

BUT WHY ARE MORE LEADERS NEEDED?

They're needed because God uses leaders to make the vision

become a reality. God could do it all by himself, but he chooses to do his work through people. When God gives a vision, there is a part he plays, and there is a part people play as well.

We tell those at CenterSet that perhaps part of the reason God has sent them to Silicon Valley at this time is because he wants them to play a part in helping us accomplish the vision he has given our church.

Please note: In the process of reading this book, you might discover I'm a novice to leadership. I'm not writing this book because I'm the expert; I'm writing this book to *become* the expert. The process of writing a book changes you. I'm writing this book for my church, and if it blesses you, great! I would love to hear more ideas about how to improve as a leader and welcome you to contact me:

Ali Roohi
ALI@CENTERSET.CHURCH

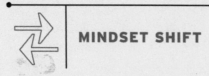

MINDSET SHIFT

For the church to change, I much first change.

RECOMMENDED READING

- ○ *Crash the Chatterbox* by Steven Furtick
- ○ *Daring Greatly* by Brené Brown

The Problem with Your Church

WHAT'S THE PROBLEM WITH YOUR CHURCH?

Several years ago I had the privilege of being mentored in a cohort by a pastor named Chip Ingram, who's a hero of mine. (Check out his ministry, Walk through the Word.) The first day of the cohort, he explained he knows firsthand the difficulties of leading small churches with a congregation of 25, 50, or 85. Every size church you can think of, he's been a part of.

Most of the people in the cohort were either stuck in their ministries or their churches were shrinking. All of us needed help, and I hadn't even started a church yet.

The first exercise he asked us to do was write down the three *biggest* issues in our church. Was it a lack of money? Was it a lack of a building, or a terrible worship leader? Was it the old lady who just has to run the women's Bible studies, or was it the youth leader who dresses like a homeless person? He promised over the next several weeks he could help fix that problem no matter what it was.

So now I'll ask you. What's the biggest issue in your church?

Chip even had us go around and share our biggest problem. The answers were predictable: lack of leaders, no youth, worship being an issue, no building. Then Chip asked us to throw away the piece of paper. I was thinking, "This is so spiritual. I love it!" Then I asked, "Why?"

His answer silenced the room.

"Because those aren't the biggest problems in your church," he said. "You think they are, but they aren't. *You're the biggest problem in your church.* Your leadership hasn't moved the people through that problem yet."

Your answer reveals more about you than it does about that issue, Chip went on to explain. Your leadership either created, tolerated, or perpetuated that issue. Your answer reveals what you think is the issue in your church, but the mirror tells you what's the biggest issue in your church. Your issue isn't really your issue. How you see your issues is your issue. Why? *Because for a church to change you must change.*

Mic drop.

You are the biggest problem in your church.

Lack of resources? You.
Lack of leaders? You.
Lack of quality worship? You.
Lack of building? You.
Lack of technology? You.
Lack of volunteers? You.

Before you stop reading, let me tell you the good news.

You can change.

You can grow.

You can change how you do ministry,

You can change how your recruit volunteers.

You can change how you build leadership in your church.

You can change—meaning your church can change. But your church will never grow beyond your leadership. What Chip was trying to convince us was this simple principle: *Change the Pastor, Change the Church.*

Craig Groeschel, pastor of the largest church in America, says there are three words that should never be part of any church leader's vocabulary: *Our people won't.*

Why? Because any time we say some version of the forbidden phrase, we're casting blame. Great leaders never blame. A great leader always takes responsibility. This is a mindset shift you need. The problem with your church is *you!* Remember: change the pastor, change the church.

YOU'RE NOT ALONE

Moses had this problem too. After leading over a million Israelites out of the bondage of slavery in Egypt, these people now needed help handling domestic disputes. With no central government agency or judicial system, Moses became the cop, judge, and system. In Exodus, Moses' father-in-law Jethro came to see the chaos and lovingly asked a probing question:

When his father-in-law saw all that Moses was doing for the people, he said, "What is this you are doing for the people? Why do you alone sit as judge, while all these people stand around you from morning till evening?" Moses answered him, "Because the people come to me to seek God's will. Whenever they have a dispute, it is brought to me, and I decide between the parties and inform them of God's decrees and instructions." Moses' father-in-law replied, "What you are doing is not good. You and these people who come to you will only wear yourselves out. The work is too heavy for you; you cannot handle it alone.

(Exodus 18:14-18)

Notice how Moses responded: "Because the people come to me." Or as Pastor Craig would point out, Moses is basically saying, "My people won't."

Thankfully Jethro spoke wisdom and leadership sense into Moses, allowing him to grow and the nation of Israel to flourish.

For a church, organization, or nation to change, the leaders must first change. Your problems are not your problems—how your see your problems is your problem. Your church can change, because you can change!

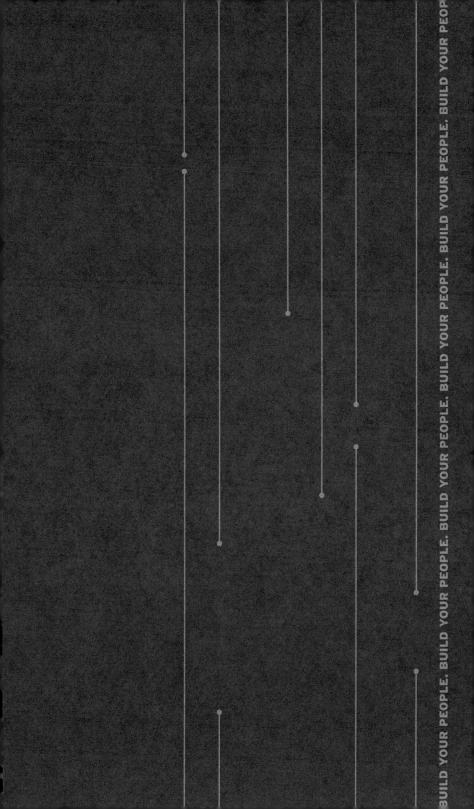

MINDSET SHIFT

I am, *therefore* I do!

RECOMMENDED READING

○ *Sun Stand Still* by Steven Furtick
○ *LeaderSight* by Jurgen Matthesius

You're Full of It!

In the winter of 2016, after passing my church planting assessment, I was on an emotional high for nearly three months. I was ready to storm the gates of hell! But before I had even started I was ready to quit. (Yes, I'm a bit of a drama king.)

I had emailed nearly 30 pastors in my community to meet for lunch or coffee, as I was about to start a new church in their backyard. Twenty of them ignored me and never responded. I met with nine of them and all of them tried to get me to stop planting and instead join them as a campus pastor or a teaching pastor.

All nine of them.

Talk about a punch in the gut. I remember wanting to quit right then and there. But I took my pain to God in prayer, and he spoke. I sensed him saying, "Ali, why are you complaining about what I'm allowing?"

My response? "What?! Why are you allowing this? That doesn't even make sense, God. *Why?*"

His answer was shocking. *Because they see something in you that you don't see in yourself. They believe in you, but you don't believe in you.*

He was right (of course). My assessment revealed that other

pastors believe in my calling and my ability to start a church with my wife, but the problem was I didn't believe in my calling. I was full of it—full of lies about myself.

You need to know you're full of it, too. That's right: you're full of lies. Lies that are holding you back from the transformation God wants to do in you, your leadership, and ultimately your church.

Other religions will make honest attempts to change people by challenging their behavior. However, when God attempts to transform people, he does this through a relationship and therefore primarily changes their identity. Why? God understands that activity flows from identity. Change someone's identity and how they see themselves and the world, and they will behave differently.

For example, imagine you're looking for a new water source at the base of a mountain. If you find a stream with water that's flowing red because of minerals, you don't clear the water at the bottom of the mountain, because red water will continue to flow down. You don't change downstream issues, but you change them upstream, at the source. In the same way, your identify is the source of you! The things you do are just the downstream issue.

Even the secular world understands this principle. In the Disney movie *Lion King,* Simba was living Hakuna Matata, their version of YOLO. He didn't change his activity until an encounter with his murdered father reminded him of *who* he really was.

In the same way, gyms, businesses, and clothing companies are no longer calling people to do but to be. If you don't believe me, just look up any social media influence and they are telling people who they are, not just what to do. For example, "You are strong" or "You are..." Activity flows from identity.

This is what leaders need to understand. The problem with their church is *them,* and it's because they don't see themselves the way God, our heavenly Father, sees us!

When God wanted to change Abram's activity, he changed his name from Abram ("high father") to Abraham ("father of a multitude"). In doing so, God was changing how Abraham saw himself, and his habits, behavior patterns, and mindsets. Abraham wasn't his past failures, his mistakes, or his lack of fruit. Even though he wasn't yet a father, God wanted to transform his thinking and help him see himself as one. This is the concept of "identify before identity."

We know that Abraham began to take this to heart because of a story found in Genesis 20, where Abraham pimps his wife Sarah out to a man named Abimelek. Unaware Sarah is Abraham's wife, Abimelek takes her into his harem, until God intervenes. Abimelek learns the truth, rebukes our father of faith and the whole mess is cleared up. Then something happens that many people overlook:

> Then Abraham prayed to God, and God healed Abimelech, his wife, and his female servants, so they could have children.
> (*Genesis 20:17*)

Did you catch that? Abraham prays for a nation to have children when he can't have children of his own. This man's identify had so been transformed that he was blessing people with a blessing he didn't yet possess. That's a perfect picture of identity changing activity. The only way to give what you don't have is by faith, when God has so changed your identity you can't help but operate in it.

This is what God wants to do in you! He wants to change how you do ministry, by changing how you see yourself.

These twelve declarations come from Steven Furtick's book *Sun Stand Still*. They will challenge how you see yourself and change your identity to how God sees you. Each declaration is backed with Scripture:

1. I am fully forgiven and free from all shame and condemnation (*Romans 8:1-2, Ephesians 1:7-8, 1 John 1:9*).

2. I act in audacious faith to change the world in my generation (*Joshua 10:12-14, John 14:12*).

3. I have no fear or anxiety; I trust in the Lord with all of my heart (*Proverbs 3:5-6, Philippians 4:6-7, 1 Peter 5:7*).

4. I am able to fulfill the calling God has placed on my life (*Exodus 3:9-12, Psalm 57:2, Colossians 1:24-29*).

5. I am fully resourced to do everything God has called me to do (*Deuteronomy 8:18, Luke 6:38, Philippians 4:13*).

6. I have no insecurity, because I see myself the way God sees me (*Genesis 1:26-27, Psalm 139:13-16, Ephesians 5:25-27*).

7. I am a faithful spouse and a godly parent—our family is blessed (*Deuteronomy 6:6-9, Ephesians 5:22-25, Colossians 3:18-19, 1 Peter 3:1-7*).

8. I am completely whole—physically, mentally, and emotionally (*Psalm 103:1-5, Matthew 8:16-17, 2 Corinthians 5:17, 1 Peter 2:24*).

9. I am increasing in influence and favor the kingdom of God (*Genesis 45:4-8, 1 Samuel 2:26, Acts 2:37-47*).

10. I am enabled to walk in the sacrificial love of Christ (*2 Thessalonians 2:16-17, 1 John 3:16; 4:9-12*).

11. I have the wisdom of the Lord concerning every decision I make (*2 Chronicles 1:7-12, Proverbs 2:6, Ecclesiastes 2:26, James 1:5*).

12. I am protected from all harm and evil in Jesus' name (*Genesis 50:20, Psalm 3:1-3, 2 Thessalonians 3:2-3*).

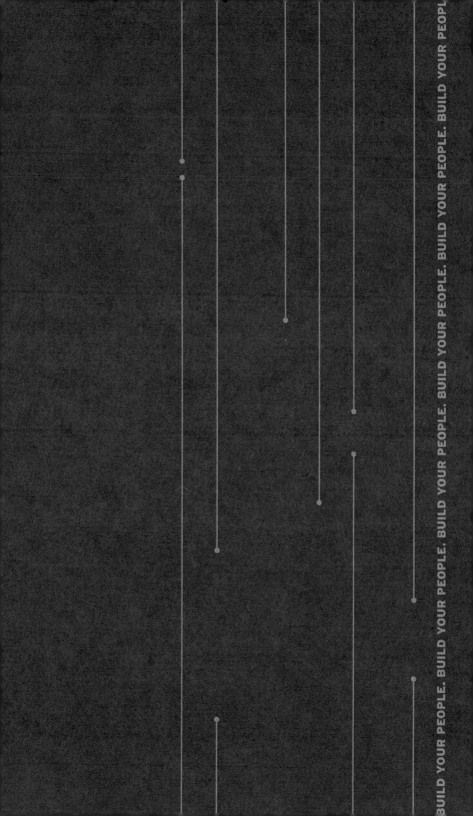

MINDSET SHIFT

My problems are not my problem—how I see my problems is my problem.

RECOMMENDED READING

- *Natural Church Development* by Christian Schwarz
- *Empowering Leadership* by Michael Fletcher
- *Leadership and Church Size Dynamics* by Tim Keller

03

Break Up or Break Down

Did you know?

- 95% of all churches in America are under 350 people
- 60% of all churches in America are under 100 people

According to Thom S. Rainer, one of the key reasons most churches do not move beyond 350 in average worship attendance is they do not have sufficient leadership and structures in place.

Most leaders don't think like leaders. In fact, most senior pastors think a medium church is just a larger version of a small church. It's not! Everything is different. How churches communicate, recruit, prepare for events, and make decisions changes. Everything is different.

But the secret of church growth is not making growth the main goal. The focus needs to be on growing people and releasing them into ministry. This is what it means to have a leadership development mindset. Effective leadership is key for growth to occur. Simply put, it is what good leaders naturally do that produces and sustains growth!

Good leaders focus on strategy to break through growth barriers. Great leaders focus on leadership to break though growth barriers.

Breaking growth barriers is less about changing the church and more about changing your mindset.

LIE #1: "IF ONLY WE HAD..."

I've never met Pastor Tommy Barnett, but his life has impacted me greatly. He once said, "Everything you need to reach your city is already in the house." While most pastors focus on what they don't have, God focuses on what we *do* have.

Take the story found in John 2, where Jesus turns water into wine at a wedding party. (Ain't no party like a Jesus party! Even unbelievers know and love this story.) Jesus asks the servants to fill three 60-gallon water jugs full of water. In a time when there was no public water system, this was an enormous request. This wasn't five to ten minutes worth of work, but likely hours, as the servants had to walk to the city well with empty water buckets and walk back with heavy ones.

Through this remarkable miracle, God teaches us several principles. I love preaching this story because it's a great church planting parable. Do the hard work that Jesus asks, and watch what he can do with it. Or put another way, when we do ordinary things, God can do extraordinary things.

Notice that God didn't provide any materials supernaturally. He worked with what the servants had. Did you catch that? He used what was already in the house. Or as Tommy puts it, "Everything you need to reach your city is already in the house." That's why you don't need a new LED wall, a new building, or even new people. You need God!

LIE #2: "I MUST BE GREAT AT EVERYTHING."

This is the lie deep in the heart of the superstar pastor who is smart, extremely hard working, and naturally gifted in many areas. This lie is difficult to reject because everything you touch excels and gets better. But eventually (if you're not there already) you will become the bottleneck to your church's growth.

One of my mentors, Pastor Steve Stroope from Lake Pointe Church in Dallas, Texas, taught me that there are four categories that we can use to break down the things we should and shouldn't do:

Bad: These are things you shouldn't do because you're terrible at them. Think of the first two weeks of American Idol: every contestant thinks they are the next Whitney Houston or Mariah Carey, yet everyone in the audience is laughing. No one takes them seriously because they're so bad. Likewise, there are things you simply shouldn't do because there isn't an ounce of talent in your body to do them. (And that's OK, by the way.)

Good: These are things you're decent at, but no one will pay you to do them. Maybe that's playing the guitar, mowing your lawn, or cleaning your house. You're good enough for you, but not enough for others to pay you to do these things.

Great: These are the things you excel at. You could easily make a career from the stuff you do in this selection. This list should be short and sweet. For me this is engineering. I made six figures for 15 years as a software engineer. I can solve problems, and I am good at it.

God: There is very little difference between the great and God categories, except for one thing. When you're doing that "thing" God has wired you to do, it gives you energy, while the great thing simply drains you. For me, leading is my God thing, and I'm great at engineering, but when I work as a software engineer, I get drained and tired. People will pay me to do it, but I feel exhausted afterwards. I would lead for free even though I excel at it! That's the difference.

Too many leaders try to be great at everything. Their behavior is actually ignoring God, even though they are doing ministry for him. They ignore his design, his plans, and his gifting in themselves and in others.

That's why you need to figure out your unique abilities and contributions. Where can you make the biggest impact? If you buy into the myth that you need to be great at everything, you will give energy to improving a skill when you could be looking for a person who is better than you to fulfill that task. There are things you are great at that others hate, and there are things you hate and someone else on your team excels at.

Choose to focus your energy on the few things you believe God has called you to do, and improve in those areas.

LIE #3: "I CAN'T IMPROVE OR GET BETTER."

Listen: growth is possible if you adopt a growth mindset! Your belief about growth (either positive or negative) will become a self-fulfilling prophecy.

Most likely the root of this lie is a fear of failure. You're afraid to fail. Let me help you remember that when something doesn't work, you don't fail; you simply learn what doesn't work. Someone with a "fixed" mindset, on the other hand, doesn't want to experience failure. They would rather stick with something they know and do well in order to not be labeled a failure. In fact, they will choose the less challenging path so they can continue to support their own notion of "being good" at whatever it is. A person with a fixed mind-set would rather not take a risk at all than look like a failure to the outside world.

Think about the sports world. After 13 years the great Kobe Bryant was still calling mentors to learn new tricks. His mentoring session with Hakeem Olajuwon went viral because he was already a five-time NBA champion, and a two-time MVP. Church leaders should take notice. We should think about leadership like a professional athlete thinks about their sport. They are constantly trying to improve their game. So here's the lesson: get better by identifying specific skills within your craft and work on them for a period of time.

All the results in your church are because of you: how you lead, how your delegate, and how you develop others. Let me say it again: if you want your church to change, you must change. You can change, meaning your church can change. But your church will never grow beyond your leadership.

Now let's take a look at three truths you need to embrace in order to change your mindset.

TRUTH #1: EVERYONE IN YOUR CHURCH HAS A PART TO PLAY.

Why has God given *you* a big vision for your church? It might surprise you, but it's not about you. It's not even about God, because God could do the whole thing himself without your help. God has given you vision for your church because his vision is, was, and will always be about *his people*. God's vision is always for God's people.

If you're not a senior pastor, don't join a church unless the vision of the church is too big for that church. Why? Because otherwise they won't need you. Real biblical vision will call things out of you, and you will be asked to do things you've never done before.

Churches with a big vision are constantly promoting and pulling others up to help.

Everyone in your church is called to ministry. *You* are called to equip them. This means you're not called to do the ministry, but to equip others to do ministry. Building people is your job. This will never happen unless you embrace the truth that everyone in your church has a part to play. You have to believe God has a calling on their lives!

The goal is not to attract people to serve you and your vision. Again, the vision isn't about you. You're called to find, stir-up, and draw out people's talents. God's vision was never about one person, because the Bible says that those in the church are all Spirit filled. Every believer is a minister, called into the royal priesthood.

The church in America is small because pastors minister and people lead. Yet the biblical model is that people minister and pastors lead.

TRUTH #2: YOU NEED TO BELIEVE MORE FOR OTHERS.

If most pastors struggle with identity issues, I can promise you everyone in your church does too! Most don't believe in themselves. They need to know someone other than God actually believes in them. They're wondering, "Does anyone think God has a place of significance for me?"

I remember in 2016 when I sat down with one of my best friends, Will Guillen, to discuss his role in helping start CenterSet. I'll never forget his first question: "Ali, do you really think I can help you? Come on. I have nothing to offer." What an honest question! I remember looking at him and saying, "YES, YES! God wants to use you and he will."

Over the next six months before we launched, Will came to

every launch team meeting. He was always quietly observing and participating. Then two weeks before our grand opening we handed out invite cards and asked everyone to pray about inviting five people. Will took over 100 cards. I remember saying, "Will, those cost money, bro!" He assured me he would put them to good use.

On the day of our grand opening, thirty of Will's co-workers came to our church. Two of them accepted Christ! The person who didn't think God could use him became the Billy Graham of our church. I remember thinking, *Are you kidding! Only God!* I asked Will, "What did you do?" Little did I know each night he packed UPS trucks for the morning shift of deliveries, so he put the invite cards in over 100 UPS trucks.

The people God sends to your church are a gift. They need to know that someone other than God believes in them! Do you truly believe *anyone* in your church is gifted and empowered to change your city? If you do, empower them to lead. Take the risk!

TRUTH #3: YOUR CHURCH'S LEADERS SHOULD BE BUILT IN HOUSE.

When I was in seminary at Shiloh Bible College in Oakland, California, I spoke with the founder, Pastor Violet Kiteley. This woman had the greatest faith of anyone I've ever met. How did a woman in her sixties, without a husband, start a church that now reaches thousands? I once asked her, "What's the greatest advice you would give a young leader hoping to build a church from scratch?"

Her answer shocked me: "Build your leaders in house." She said my job as senior pastor was to discover, develop, and deploy others to do the work of the ministry.

Chris Hodges, senior pastor of Church of the Highlands, echoes this sentiment when he says, "Make equipping people the main function of the people on staff! Not doing ministry, but equipping."

Here are some questions to honestly answer:

- How does your church build leaders?
- How does a non-believer in your church begin serving?
- How does someone who is serving with potential take the next step to lead?
- How does someone who is a leader of others take more responsibility and lead a ministry?

If those steps aren't clear for you, it won't be clear for others either. You must move from a doer to a delegator. You need to train yourself out of a job, because when you do a job for others in the church, you're actually robbing others of ministry opportunities and the chance to learn and grow.

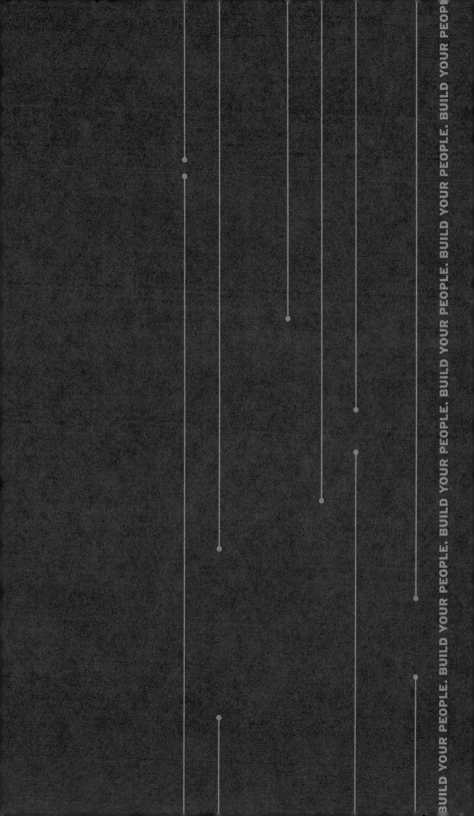

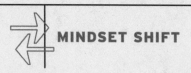

MINDSET SHIFT

The hardest person to lead in any organization is always you!

RECOMMENDED READING

- *Spiritual Leadership* by John Oswald Sanders
- *Emotionally Healthy Spirituality* by Peter Scazzero
- *Leaders Who Last* by Dave Kraft
- *Atomic Habits* by James Clear
- *Good to Great* by Jim Collins

The Hardest Person to Lead

Who's the hardest person to lead in any church?

Is it the lazy youth leader?
Is it the crazy old woman who's led the same ministry for fifty years?
Is it the stubborn elders who want the good old days?
Who's the hardest person to lead in your church?

You are.

It's always the person in the mirror. You're the most stubborn person. You're the biggest critic, the most vocal antagonist. All leadership begins with self-leadership, because leading yourself is the hardest thing to do.

Here are two self-leadership principles to help you grow in your leadership:

1. The best **leaders** are the best **followers**.
2. A leader is **measured** by their **habits** and daily **disciplines**.

Let's break this down.

PRINCIPLE #1: THE BEST LEADERS ARE THE BEST FOLLOWERS.

Before we lead others, we need to make sure we are centering our entire lives around Jesus.

For example, take the biblical characters Abraham and Lot, who both left their homeland to follow God and pursue his promise. Yet when you count how many times each of them built an altar of worship to Jesus, you find the true mark of their leadership. Both were called to leadership, yet only one of them had great self-leadership.

Instead of focusing on your church changing, you should always focus on how you first need to change. So where do you struggle as a leader? What areas of your life are constantly broken but ignored? What private part of your life would you be embarrassed if others saw and were asked to evaluate? Great leaders self-identify these areas and ask God to transform them. Better check yourself before you wreck yourself.

> O Lord, you have searched me and known me!
> (*Psalm* 139:1)

Begin with a time of self-evaluation. Stop and be still before the Lord. Thank him, praise him, and worship him! Now ask him where you need to grow—not for self-glory but so that you can become more like Jesus. The by-product of you pursuing Jesus is leading others well.

Questions to consider:

- How am I passionately pursing Christ?

- What's the health of my marriage?
- How physical healthy am I?
- What is my level of integrity?
- How easily am I offended?
- How well do I model generosity?
- Where is there a lack of health in my life?

If you need more help knowing what areas of your life to evaluate, this list from a dear mentor of mine, Pastor Steve Stroope, can help you:

1. Fit
   - **Physical:** sleep, diet, exercise
   - **Mental:** books, skills, constant learning, rest
   - **Spiritual:** relationship with God, spiritual disciplines
   - **Relational:** interactions, mentorship, iron sharpening iron (*Proverbs 27:17*)
2. Faithful
   - **Marriage:** growing in love, friendship, faithful to spouse
   - **Parenting:** grace, discipline
   - **Finances:** good stewardship
   - **Career:** good employee
3. Fruitful
   - **The Lost:** leading others to Christ
   - **Influence:** Paul-Timothy relationship—who are you pouring into?

PRINCIPLE #2: A LEADER IS MEASURED BY THEIR HABITS AND DAILY DISCIPLINES.

In his book *Good to Great*, Jim Collins tells the true story of two teams racing nearly a century ago to the reach the South Pole. Each team (we'll call them Team A and Team B) kept journals and recorded their daily travels, allowing us to learn some amazing leadership principles.

Team A traveled when the weather was good. They would say things in their journal like, "Today we traveled 50 miles, because the sun was out." Other days they would say the weather was terrible, so they only traveled five miles. Some days they didn't even move because the weather was so bad!

Every day their journal was recorded, Team B traveled 20 miles. They would say, "We could have gone more but we didn't." Or, "We didn't want to travel that far, but we had to." Rain or shine, sun or blizzard, team B traveled 20 miles. Every single day! That's leadership.

Team A got to the South Pole first, but ultimately they died before returning.

What's the lesson? If you want to lead others, you must first lead yourself, daily.

So what's your 20 mile march? What are the daily habits you do every single day?

Here are mine:

- 30 minutes alone with God each day (This is not sermon prep.)
- 1 hour each day reading a leadership book
- Work out three to four times a week
- No more than 15 minute on social media each day
- Fast 24 hours each week to beat my flesh and hear the voice of God clearly

I'll ask you again. *What's your 20 mile march?* What are the things you do to build yourself? To transform people, we first must first be deeply transformed ourselves.

Like an iceberg, only 10% our life is above the water and visible to others, meaning 90% of who we really are is beneath the water. These are the areas of our life that are often untouched by Jesus and only healthy spiritual habits (what I call your 20 mile march) will touch and change these areas. We need to be deeply transformed beneath the surface.

HOW DO YOU DEFINE SPIRITUAL DISCIPLINES?

These are deliberately self-imposed actions that enter our existing life and thought patterns in order to foster spiritual growth and lead us to maturity. They not the end goal of a spiritual life, but the means to get there. To be a discipline, it needs to be intentional and frequent.

WHAT'S THE IMPORTANCE OF SPIRITUAL DISCIPLINES?

They are called "disciplines" because they don't come naturally. You need to make a conscious choice to engage in them. There will be times when you don't feel like doing them, but you do them anyway because you know they are necessary for your spiritual health. The disciplines give you structure and order, because otherwise you would ignore your spiritual health.

Relational intimacy with Christ is reinforced when we engage in the disciplines. Intimacy with God must be intentional because it never happens by chance. We purposefully perform spiritual disciplines because we seek greater intimacy with God and desire to be more like him.

WHAT ARE THE SPIRITUAL DISCIPLINES?

1. **Prayer:** Prayer is simply talking with God. However, prayer changes us inwardly, making us instruments of God's grace. Prayer is to faith, what research is science. To pray is to change. Prayer is the central avenue that God uses to transform us

2. **Scripture:** Jesus said when you know the truth, the truth will set you free. Knowing the truth is foundational for a follower of Jesus and sets you on the path for freedom! Remember, don't just read your Bible; *spend time with Jesus.* At CenterSet we teach the S.O.A.P. approach to reading and studying Scripture.

3. **Meditation:** God transforms us primarily by the renewing of our minds. When we begin to think God's thoughts, we make decisions like God would. Wisdom isn't built in a day, but it is built daily. Mediation is about prayerfully pondering the Word of God with the aid of the Holy Spirit. The most powerful method of meditation is Scripture memorization! If you can remember Post Malone songs, you can remember Jesus songs too!

4. **Fasting:** This is the practice of intentionally denying and controlling our physical desires and sensitivity in order to increase our spiritual strength. If prayer connects you with God, fasting disconnects you from the world. When you fast and pray regularly, you're enhancing your spiritual sensitivity and strength.

Leading yourself is the most difficult leadership challenge. Your personal life shapes the health and culture of the teams you lead. If you're serious about leadership, you must lead yourself!

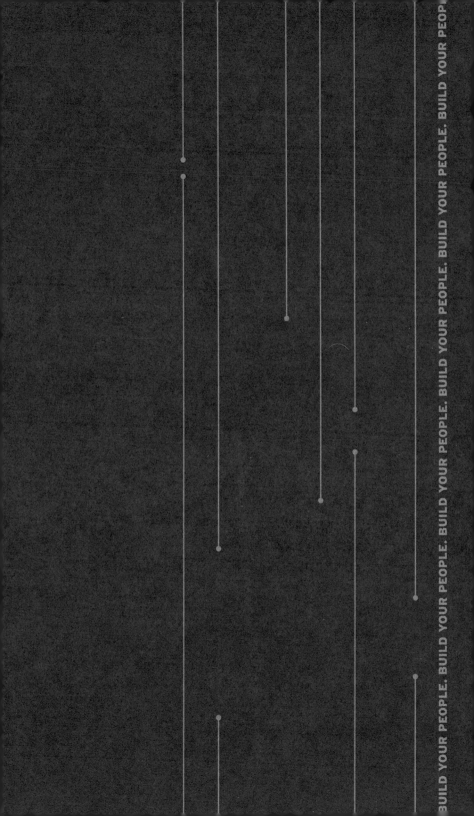

MINDSET SHIFT

If you don't clearly define leadership, others will define it for you.

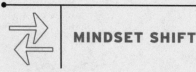

RECOMMENDED READING

- *Culture Wins* by William Vanderbloemen
- *An Unstoppable Force* by Erwin McManus
- *The Culture Code* by Daniel Coyle
- *Cracking Your Church's Culture Code* by Sam Chand
- *Canoeing the Mountains* by Tod Bolsinger
- *The Secret* by Ken Blanchard and Mark Millar

05

Define Who a Leader Is

How do we define leadership? It's important we share the same definition because culture is created by language. For example, at CenterSet we don't have volunteers—we have leaders. Volunteers do a task; leaders have a God-given calling. We believe that since everyone has some level of influence, everyone has leadership potential.

We'll talk more about culture later, but it's vital we understand that our language can unify us or divide us. You must define what a leader is at your church so that everyone has the same definition. Otherwise, if you ask one hundred leaders in your church, you'll probably get one hundred different definitions and answers for leadership. If you want to reproduce the right kind of leader, you must first define leadership, then communicate and celebrate it! We took our definition straight from the book *Empowering Leadership*, which in turn took it from Chick-fil-A. Please take it from us!

THE POWER OF LANGUAGE

> "The LORD said, 'If they have begun to do this as one people all having the **same language**, then nothing they plan to do will be **impossible** for them."
> (*Genesis 11:6*)

One language created powerful unity for these people. While they used this unity for evil purposes, this verse speaks to the power of a group of people focused in the same direction, speaking the same language, and passionate about the same goals. Imagine a church a staff team with one mission, all speaking the same language? Imagine a dream team with one goal, one heartbeat, empowered by the same Spirit? That would be powerful! Imagine an entire church united and passionate for their local community? They would be unstoppable!

So stop and ask yourself:

- Do the people at your church talk alike?
- Do they all use the same phrases?

Singular language creates movement in a singular direction!

WHAT'S THE DEFINITION OF A LEADER AT CENTERSET?

True leadership has nothing to do with a person's title or position. There are many people who display and exemplify leadership without official titles and leadership positions. Instead, leadership is characterized by two main things: doing, and being. Doing is best illustrated by skills and being is by defined by character.

Many believe they can become great leaders if they have the right skills, while others only focus on their character. But both will fail to reach a higher height in leadership because a leader needs both! The best organizations select, develop, and promote people who have both skill *and* character.

The key to great leadership is that great leaders serve. Good leaders serve others and aren't self-serving in their motivation to lead. A person can serve without leading, but a leader can't lead without serving. The best leaders serve others.

The S.E.R.V.E acronym explains there are five key ways leaders serve through their ongoing actions. The language of S.E.R.V.E demands strong and decisive leadership, but it also assumes that the fundamental role of a leader is to serve others and help them become better, not merely to move them from one place to another for organizational gain.

SEE THE FUTURE

"S" is about your vision as the leader for the future of your group, team, or organization. This vision gives the team passion and direction.

Great leaders don't just talk about the "what"; they clearly see and communicate the "why." Seeing and casting compelling vision is the mark of a leader versus someone who is merely a doer.

Good leaders solve problems. Great leaders solve problems before others know they exist or see them. Whether the issue is people, money, volunteers, parking, or kids, great leaders look ahead and see issues before they happen.

The key is to not be so busy that you can't look to the future. You need self-leadership to carve out time to look ahead. Great leaders use tools, software, and resources to foster future growth and fore-see problems.

ENGAGE AND DEVELOP OTHERS

It's the leader's job to ensure not only that you have the right people on your team, but also that they are serving in the right roles.

Everything you do as a leader hinges on the people around you. You must find, recruit, develop, and empower others. This is the highest and most important role of a leader. Leaders still do work, but they mainly do the work through others.

Great leaders select and develop other leaders because the cost of poor selection is too high. Everyone hates having a poor performing team member who isn't carrying their own weight. This kills morale and over the long term, will hinder team performance. That's why the best organizations have a very strict hiring process. They hire slow and fire fast.

But once you select the right people, you invest in developing leaders because you understand that you can't do it all. Wise leaders delegate and develop others.

REINVENT CONTINUALLY

Great leaders have a natural distain for the status quo. This starts with getting better on a personal level, because if you stop learning, you stop leading. So ask yourself:

- What books am I reading?
- Who am I learning from? (Not just books but mentors)
- Who is further along than me in my current role that I can learn from?

Show me a leader who is reading two books a month and regularly meeting with mentors, and I'll show you a growing church.

Natural Church Development studied thousands of churches,

and found that the number one quality of a growing church across *all denominations* was whether the church was willing to learn from others. Proverbs shows how highly God values wisdom and our seeking it. So how desperately are you seeking wisdom versus a bigger paycheck? If you can't take criticism, you're not a learner.

Leaders of growing churches are learners! One way they seek to get better is on an operations level: systems and processes. Leaders must instill a desire to get better or improve how we do day-to-day to work. They can ask their team:

- Is there a better way to do what we normally do?
- How can we do this faster, better, or more efficiently?
- What are we doing that can improve?

Leaders also get better on a structural level. They analyze their organization and ask:

- Is our structure built to sustain our growth?
- Is our structure a bottleneck to our future plans and growth?

VALUE RELATIONSHIPS AND RESULTS

Sometimes the corporate world is only about results. But at the same time, sometimes the non-profit church world can only be about relationship. Both are wrong. You need both!

The best leaders raise the bar on excellence and make very high demands, yet at the same time they have good relationships with those they lead. They provide both challenge and support through their leadership.

John Maxwell says that people will not give your their hands until they can see your heart. This means people's best work will only arrive after they see that you really care about them. Great leaders intimately know their team members on a personal level, and yet push their team to grow.

EMBODY THE VALUES

Great leaders create, communicate, model, and correct core values. But they don't just communicate values and culture; they embody them and live them out.

Being is more important than communicating because more is caught than taught from leaders. Embodying the values of the organization builds credibility and trust among team members.

Great leadership is more about being than doing.

S.E.R.V.E LEADERSHIP EVALUATION QUESTIONS

S   How many times each week/month do I look to see and understand the future?

E   How many times each week/month do I engage and develop others?

R   How many times each week/month do I assess my current situation and look to reinvent?

V   How many times each week/month do I work to purposefully value both relationships and results?

E   How many times each week/month do I consciously embody the values of my organization?

Finally, it's vital that we understand that leaders are very different than managers. This isn't a book on management, but on leadership.

In his book *Cracking Your Church's Culture Code*, Sam Chand explains the differences between leaders and managers:

Leaders	Managers
Conceptualize outcome by working from the future back to the present	Conceptualize plans by working from the past to the present
Embrace a macro — big picture — perspective	Embrace a micro — snapshot — perspective
Favor innovative thinking	Favor routine thinking
Possess revolutionary flair	Are protectors of the status quo
Emphasize the what and why	Emphasize the how and when
Are inspiring and motivating	Are controlling and directing
Are excited by change	Are threatened by change
Move quickly	Move slowly
Identify opportunities	Identify obstacles
Take risks	Avoid risks
Pursue acquisition of resources	Are bounded by available resources
Are people centered	Are system centered
Are idea centered	Are plan centered
Perceive people's approval as a want	Perceive people's approval as a need

MINDSET SHIFT

Culture influences your church more than vision and values. It is the most powerful invisible force in your church. A bad culture will consistently undermine an amazing mission, vision, and strategy.

RECOMMENDED READING

- ○ *Cracking Your Church's Culture Code* by Sam Chand
- ○ *Culture Wins* by William Vanderbloemen
- ○ *An Unstoppable Force* by Erwin McManus
- ○ *The Culture Code* by Daniel Coyle
- ○ *Canoeing the Mountains* by Tod Bolsinger

Curate Your Culture

Why is culture so important? It's been said that culture is more important than vision, but why? Because culture dictates how people respond to the vision of the organization. In a healthy culture of trust, faith, and respect, people respond with action to a vision. When that isn't happening, it's not a vision problem—it's a culture problem.

In order to build a successful organization, you first discover your *why* and define your culture, then figure out your strategy!

Many times leaders focus solely on vision to the exclusion of culture. But culture determines how we get to our destination. For example, let's say we are in San Jose, California and we want to drive a fifteen-passenger van to Denver, Colorado. Denver is the vision. It's the destination that is currently unseen but we can picture it and work towards it. But *how* we drive to Denver, what's on the radio, what's in the cooler, what kind of jokes and conversation we have along the way isn't vision but culture. Both are important but are also very different. And leaders must steward both!

What is culture? Culture is how you behave based on what you *believe*. Culture is shaped by people and language. Those who are the culture and speak the culture are called "culture carriers."

In *The Culture Code*, Daniel Coyle writes, "Culture is a set of living relationships working toward a shared goal."

The Merriam-Webster Dictionary defines culture as "The beliefs and customs of a particular group; a way of thinking, behaving, or working that exists in a place or organization."

Culture is best described as the personality of an organization. And culture is created by the collective influence of the team. It's not a system or an isolated initiative. It isn't a bunch of perks or fun stuff. (A great culture doesn't mean you love it every day!)

HOW DO WE DISCOVER OUR ORGANIZATION'S PERSONALITY?

This can be discovered by honestly asking these questions:

- Who are we?
- What do we believe?
- What do we value?
- How do we behave?

These things are expressed through: language, rituals, stories, and heroes. They are the things people accept without thinking about them.

Culture influences your church more than vision and values because every person in your organization contributes to the culture. However, leaders have a disproportionate influence on their culture. This means your church's culture exists whether you define it or not, and is being built or eroded every day. That's why the senior leader of a church or team should never ignore culture.

A positive culture of leadership is best built when you believe everyone in your church plays a part, and then is given significant ministry and challenges. It's built when people are held accountable and the standard of excellence is not lowered. It's built when leaders clearly communicate expectations and are organized.

Since more is caught than taught, culture must be modeled by leaders, communicated through language, affirmed through accountability, and celebrated for it to be reproduced in team members.

DID JESUS TEACH CULTURE?

Absolutely! We see it in when Jesus sends out the disciples two by two, and gives them a culture talk:

These twelve Jesus sent out with the following instructions: "Do not go among the Gentiles or enter any town of the Samaritans. Go rather to the lost sheep of Israel. As you go, proclaim this message: 'The kingdom of heaven has come near.' Heal the sick, raise the dead, cleanse those who have leprosy, drive out demons. Freely you have received; freely give. Do not get any gold or silver or copper to take with you in your belts—no bag for the journey or extra shirt or sandals or a staff, for the worker is worth his keep. Whatever town or village you enter, search there for some worthy person and stay at their house until you leave. As you enter the home, give it your greeting. If the home is deserving, let your peace rest on it; if it is not, let your peace return to you. If anyone will not welcome you or listen to your words, leave that home or town and shake the dust off your feet."

(Matthew 10:5-14)

Jesus teaches them to gather around a unified cause. He motivates them with encouragement and gives them instructions to follow. Then he sends them out to accomplish the mission.

He told the disciples what to carry and what to do, and taught them how to recognize receptiveness.

What culture was Jesus was teaching them? A culture of trusting God. And what would have happened if he hadn't defined the culture? Everyone disciple would have made a different definition of success. They would have had different ideas of what to do and how to do it. It would have been chaos! Who knows if anyone would have gotten saved.

We see another example of culture later in Scripture in the letter by James the brother of Jesus. In James 2, churches are instructed how to greet guests, whether rich and poor. They are to show no partiality. That's setting the culture.

EXAMPLES OF CORPORATE CULTURE DONE RIGHT

In the 1980s, **Sam Walton**, the founder of Wal-Mart, called an all hands on meeting with 100,000 employees and famously had each employee raise their right hand and swear: "From this day forward, I solemnly promise and declare that every time a customer comes within ten feet of me, I will smile, look him in the eye, and greet him, so help me Sam."

Disney models setting culture through the use of language:

- Employees are "cast members"
- Customers are "guests"
- A crowd is an "audience"
- A work shift is a "performance"
- A job is a "part"
- A job description is a "script"
- A uniform is a "costume"

- Being on duty is being "on stage"
- Being off duty is being "off stage"

In the 1990s **Rudy Giuliani** took office as mayor of New York City, and implemented a strategy called the "broken windows theory." It idea was to fix broken windows within 24 hours and give the signal that things are being watched and taken care of. Crime dropped 60% overall within a year!

Another example is **Pike Fish Market** in Seattle. They are known for having fun while they sell fish, as they throw fish 30 feet before bagging them for customers. They sell an experience, and this is the primary reason why they sell more fish than any other fish market.

WHAT'S A CULTURE CARRIER?

Remember everything has a culture. Your life has a culture, and so does your marriage, your home, and your business. Our churches also have a culture.

If you're a leader, it is you who sets the culture. You cannot build the culture unless you are prepared to be the culture.

So how do you do that? By building a culture around faithful people. Faithful people in your organization are the "culture carriers." They are the culture, and they speak the culture.

Notice that being a culture carrier is not based solely on skill or competency. Healthy and wise churches promote, recruit, and reward based on culture, not skill!

If you have a person with five-star culture but who only has three-star skills and talents, that person is always better for your organization than a person with five-star skills but only three-star culture. Why? Because culture gets repeated.

Culture creates unity and momentum. Culture carriers are the ones who will teach others the collective habits long after you have left. They will carry the vision and make the changes necessary to maintain the heart and purposes of your mission.

WHAT'S THE CULTURE AT CENTERSET?

To show how we've worked to establish a purposeful culture at our church, here are our core values we share with our leaders:

Ridiculous Responsiveness

We believe in setting the atmosphere wherever we go, whether that's at home, work, or church. We don't let the atmosphere affect us; we allow the Holy Spirit to set the atmosphere.

We are a loud and bold church. We model our faith not just in our prayer closet, but also in our worship experiences (both Sunday services and groups). We speak boldly because that's who we are— bold leaders.

Tenacious Teachability

We have the humility to say we don't have it all figured out. Therefore, we embrace healthy conflict and encouragement because that makes us better!

We're not afraid to say, "I need help, I need wisdom, I need insight!" We are serious about getting better. We ask questions, seek mentors, learn and grow. None of us have arrived!

Proverbs says that wisdom is more valuable than gold. So what books are you reading? What leaders are you learning from? We also come to church expecting that God is going to speak to us, and that's why we bring out notebooks.

Super Servanthood

We believe that gratitude keeps us humble and reminds us that ministry is something that we get to do, not have to. We are passionate about what we do because it's not just a job, it's a calling. It's a privilege to serve Christ and invite others! That's why we take hits and keep on going. We will not give up.

We understand that if serving is beneath you, leadership is beyond you. We serve because that's our nature as Christ followers. Jesus taught us to go the second mile (Matthew 5:41), so that's our second nature. Leaders lead with a butler towel, not a crown.

Fun Fundamentalism

Jesus started his ministry with a bar tab and hung out with children, yet he was serious about his faith to the point of death. But we shouldn't miss that he was fun and had a sense of humor. Therefore, church should be fun, a place of joy and excitement. Even though we talk about heaven and hell, the church should be attractive.

We have fun at church! We choose to be joyful and grateful even when it gets difficult.

We never take for granted what God is doing here at CenterSet Church. We constantly encourage one another publicly and lift one another up. We also are generous and give things away. Our goal isn't to create religious environments, but ones that are exciting and encouraging.

That's why we ask each other, do you believe Jesus is enjoyable? Are *you* enjoyable? Do people like being around you? Is the joy of the LORD really your strength?

As a leader, one way I encourage this is by planning humor in my messages and team talks. We all need to laugh more!

Heartfelt Honor

This is important for every organization! Honor means "to put weight on." The culture of honor is about putting weight on people, things, and God. You cannot receive from that which you do not honor!

In Hebrews 13, God's Word says to honor your leaders. We are a causal church in that people can come as they are, but we are not casual in honor with our leaders. Biblical honor is given not earned!

Honor up and down, and side to side. Honor prays, respects, and rallies around the vision of the house. It also corrects in private, and praises others in public. This isn't a "yes" man culture.

Public loyalty leads to being a private influencer.

HOW TO CELEBRATE CULTURE?

When celebrating culture, don't celebrate individual people but the cultural value you see in them. You want to promote the culture in people, not their skill!

For example:

> "Hey everyone, I want to celebrate 'people are our priority'! I saw Jessica go out of her way to help a first-guest church check their children in Kids Church and then she walked that same couple to the bathroom because they were lost!"

Always remember that the culture is great than individual people. This ensures that the team is greater than any one person.

THE HIDDEN POWER OF CULTURE

The Harvard Business Review often states that in general people don't leaves jobs; they leave managers. Likewise, people don't leave pastors or churches; they leave cultures. So is your church's culture healthy or toxic?

However, sometimes even if the culture is crystal clear and

healthy, people will still leave. It might sound harsh, but if they won't adjust to your culture, it's better if they leave. (Again, this is why when you're hiring, you need to ensure that people are a fit to your organization's culture, not just highly skilled.)

HOW DO YOU ASSESS YOUR CHURCH'S CULTURE?

These questions, provided by a great leader named Jenni Catron, will help you understand the current culture of your church:

1. Do we have clear, shared expectations?
2. How well do we communicate?
3. How do we handle bad news?
4. Are we vulnerable with each other? Is vulnerability modeled by leadership?
5. How do we handle disagreements?
6. Do we have our own language/vernacular?
7. Does work get done when the leader is not present?
8. Do we regularly and consistently do performance reviews?
9. Do we create and resource personal development plans for employees?

MINDSET SHIFT

The tongue has the power of life and death, and those who love it will eat its fruit (Proverbs 18:21).

RECOMMENDED READING

- The Bible
- By Design or Default? by Kevin Gerald
- Axiom by Bill Hybels
- "Lost in Translation," from The Wall Street Journal
- The Advantage by Patrick Lencioni
- Church Unique by Will Mancini

Say It,
Don't Spray It

In their book *Building a Discipleship Culture*, Mike Breen and Steve Cockram write, "Sociologists say that language creates culture....The idea that language creates culture may sound strange, but it's quite intuitive when we start to see it all around us."

Language matters—in organizations, in churches, and in families. It's been said that "words create worlds," and as leaders, the language we use helps shape the cultures we lead.

Stephen Blandino writes,*

Words frame culture. Every word you speak has bene-fits and baggage. For example, what comes to mind when you hear the following words: crusade, outreach, preacher, committee, small group, choir, band, offering, or missional? If you're leading a non-profit, what do you think of when you hear these words: volunteers, fundraising, value-added, bench-marking, advocate, mission, or stakeholders? Every word con-jures a different emotional reaction—some life-giving, others deflating—each different for every person.

* http://stephenblandino.com/2010/11/8-words-that-define-your-churchs.html

The language you choose defines your organization's culture in the minds of the people you lead and the people you serve. In Bill Hybels's book *Axioms,* he talks about how important it is to craft memorable phrases that define the goals and values of your organization. Hybels observes, "Leaders rise and fall by the language they use.... The very best leaders I know wrestle with words until they are able to communicate their big ideas in a way that captures the imagination, catalyzes action, and lifts spirits. They coin creeds and fashion slogans and create rallying cries, all because they understand that language matters."

If you want to understand your culture, make a list of the words and phrases that you and your t eam throw around most often. What baggage or benefits do those words carry? What do they mean to you? What do they mean to your volunteers and the people you serve?

The following are some examples of phrases and language that we use at CenterSet to shape our church culture.

SERMON BEFORE THE SERMON

Every church preaches two sermons, but only one is from the stage. The other is from the church's people: people in the parking lot, greeters at the door entrance, those by the coffee station. Both sermons are important, because if we don't preach the first one well, people won't want to hear the second one.

SECOND MILE, SECOND NATURE

Jesus taught this powerful culture principle: when the world expects and demands you go one mile, go the second (*Matthew 5:41*). Make the second mile your second nature.

TODAY IS SOMEONE'S FIRST DAY!

This principle is best explained by using a Joe DiMaggio story. He is most famously known for holding the longest hit streak in major league baseball—56 games straight. Yet this man was known for his hustle on every play, and never let his accomplishments change him. He was once asked why he still sprinted from the dugout to the outfield. His response? "There is always some kid who may be seeing me for the first or last time. I owe him my best."

Likewise, today is someone's first day visiting your church, so never forget it!

IT'S NOT JUST ANOTHER SUNDAY

Churches are creators of habit. Our services usually consist of three songs, a sermon, maybe another song, and a goodbye. Then repeat again in seven days. It's often easy to forget that every time we gather, God wants to do a *new* thing. If his mercies are new every morning, then every Sunday he wants to deposit something fresh and powerful into us.

That means it's not just another Sunday to go through the motions. I've learned to come to church expectant, full of faith and anticipation for God to do something in me and in the lives of others. *It's not just another Sunday.*

WE DON'T HAVE TO DO THIS—
WE *GET* TO DO THIS!

This is all about a mindset, and it goes like this: Nobody owes me anything; Jesus gave me everything. Every single thing I'm doing is a privilege and not a right. It's a privilege to serve God and to serve his people. It's a privilege to be a leader—thank you, Jesus, for choosing me!

WELCOME HOME

We hope that every person who comes to our church will hear and experience "Welcome home." We want to welcome them to a place where they belong, to a place that gathers around the broken, to a place where love resides. This is about creating an environment that is welcoming and inclusive.

COME AS YOU ARE

Christians are notorious for loving only those who believe and behave as they do. Love is only granted after you change and earn it. But what if we created environments where people were loved and felt like they belonged before they believed? What if we loved others like Jesus loves us? This is a place where we don't need to clean up and then come to God, but allowed God to be our shower. That's the heart behind the principle of "Come as you are."

YOU BELONG HERE

That includes everyone. Not some people—all people. If God died for all people, all people are welcome and everyone belongs here. There are not clicks, no special club, no secret handshake. We exist for those who aren't here. We're actually waiting for them to join us because they belong here. New people should always feel welcome.

WE ARE BETTER TOGETHER

God designed us from the very beginning to be social creatures. He knew that we would need relationships and intimacy with others in order to function the way he intended. Not only is that true of us individually, it is true of the church as a whole. I like to say, if you want to go fast, go alone, but if you want to go far, go together!

HONEST AND INSTANT

This is about how we approach feedback. Healthy organizations and teams correct quickly and instantly, and then move on without a hiccup. For example, "That's not how we do things, and that's not who we are," and five minutes later, "Are you watching the Warriors tonight?"

NEXT STEPS

No one has arrived, but everyone is getting closer to Jesus. We say, "This is my next step. What's yours?" This prevents church from becoming a social club where we hang out and no one ever changes. (If Jesus isn't changing you, maybe you're not in relationship with him!)

CELEBRATE WHAT WE WANT REPEATED

We are careful not to celebrate people because that will create a superstar culture, but we do celebrate the church values or culture within that individual person.

So what kinds of words and phrases are you intentionally using as a leader to shape your church?

MINDSET SHIFT

You must see people as who they could *become, not who they are.*

RECOMMENDED READING

- *Empowering Leadership* by Michael Fletcher
- *LeaderSight* by Jurgen Matthesius
- *Multipliers* by Liz Wiseman

08

See Others as God Does

Leadership, the kind that develops others, requires a different mindset about the people you serve. This is sort of like being able to run seven miles, but having to walk with overweight people who like to eat donuts and plod around the track.

Will you love the current version of them, just as they are?

Will you hope, pray, and dream for more for them than they do for themselves?

Will you build them up, the way God has done for you?

Spiritually speaking, Jesus is the only sinless person. He's the only person who can run a four minute mile. So although you think you're the man for running a seven minute mile, the truth is you're *way* slower and less disciplined than him. Yet he loves the current version of you. He loves you just as you are, and he still hopes, prays, and dreams more for you than you do for yourself.

You must see people as God sees them. He sees who they *could* become, not who they *are*—the same way he sees you!

A mentor of mine, Michael Fletcher, is pastor of Manna Church and the author of *Empowering Leadership*. He once taught me a principle that gets to the heart behind this idea. He calls it the Spiritual Law of Conservation, and the idea is that God does not waste anything. What we deem as worthless and broken trash, God sees as priceless. God loves to take what other people consider trash and redeem it. *This is his heart.*

In the past, the average pastor would ask, "How can this person help me fulfill my vision and build my church?" But when you have God's heart and you see people as God sees them, everything changes.

You now ask each person: "What's your calling? What's your dream? I want to help you fulfill that!"

Something crazy happens when you build people: the church gets built. Why? Because people are naturally skeptical. But when they see a leader and a church culture that is sincere and authentic, they don't want to leave!

You must see people as God sees them: who they *could* become, not who they *are*—the same way God did with you!

FROM MEN IN TROUBLE TO MIGHTY MEN

I love the way this mindset shift is demonstrated in a story from David's life:

> So David left Gath and escaped to the cave of Adullam. Soon his brothers and all his other relatives joined him there. Then others began coming—men who were in trouble or in debt or who were just discontented—until David was the captain of about 400 men.
>
> (1 Samuel 22:1-2)

Do you notice who surrounded David?

- Men who were in **trouble**....like with the law, not their mamas.
- Men who were in **debt**....like their lives weren't in order.
- Men who were **discontented**....like these are not mature, joyful God-followers.

Why is this text so amazing? Because if you look in 2 Samuel 23:8-39, the Bible records the men who surrounded David and calls them his *mighty men*. Did you catch that? The men who were first in trouble, in debt, and discontented are now the mighty men—warriors and leaders. Simply being around David, their leader, transformed them into something else. They became all that God had created them to be.

How was David able to do this? David didn't see *who* they currently were, but who they could become. He didn't judge them. He didn't speak only to their weaknesses. He didn't highlight only their failures. Rather, he saw them as God saw them. He saw their future abilities, not their current failures. David mined for gold and developed those men into their God-given potential.

This is a leadership principle for every church leader: **Great leaders are not *found*; they are formed.** This isn't a debate about whether leaders are born or created because the answer to that question is "Yes!" They are both born and created. But if your church is ever going to fulfill the Great Commission in the current cultural climate, you can't build a strategy on hiring more leaders to solve your church problems. You can't *buy* leaders; you must *build* them by seeing their potential and speaking that over them.

So how do you see the people in your church? Your attitude determines their altitude.

How do you describe them?

What do you focus on: who they currently are, or who they can become?

MINDSET SHIFT

Everyone should be discipled, but not everyone should be developed. Learn to look for the right kind of leaders.

RECOMMENDED READING

- ○ *Empowering Leadership* by Michael Fletcher
- ○ *Good to Great* by Jim Collins
- ○ *EntreLeadership* by Dave Ramsey
- ○ *20/80 Rule: Making the Shift to a Volunteer Driven Culture* by Dr. Conway Edwards

09

Pick Your Team Wisely

What's most the important resource in an organization? Is it the location, systems, culture, innovation, products, or perhaps the strategy? No. *People are.*

Why? Because the right people will always pick the right locations, develop the best strategic systems, create and sustain healthy cultures, drive innovative ideas, and design profitable products. The potential of your church rests on the strength of its people.

This is why the smartest churches hire slowly. Dave Ramsey, in his book *EntreLeadership*, talks about how they have four or more interviews with an individual over several weeks because you just don't know how each employee will pan out. Church leaders are wise to realize Jesus prayed *all night* before picking his disciples. Picking the right people is key to growing your church. You don't need the right strategy to grow your church—you need the right people!

Why is developing the right people the best strategy? Because growing churches don't buy great leaders; they *build* them. The first step is to look for the best leaders you can find. Leaders you need for your church tomorrow are probably already in your building *today*. When you invite them to use their gifts and support them with the development and training they need, the results will be incredible.

Carey Nieuwhof writes, "The truth is, great people don't randomly assemble. They are attracted by clear and compelling missions, like the mission of the church. They are challenged, nurtured, and inspired by skillful, humble, passionate leaders who have devoted their lives to a cause greater than themselves."

The key is to start where you are. Even if you think you don't have the right people in the church, be willing to humbly look around at those in your congregation. Where do you find leaders? Look around you. *They're probably already leading something*, some small business, a mom's group, maybe a local social cause. In some context somewhere, they're leading something.

Faith that you have everything to reach your city says great leaders are probably already serving in my church, but might be on the wrong team. Or they come each week and simply need to be recruited personally. You must remember that when picking the right people, leaders respond to vision but a doer will respond to need. If you don't recognize and find these great leaders in your church, someone else or some other cause or organization will and you will ultimately lose them.

What are you looking for in people? Although we defined leadership in chapter 5, here is a leadership axiom from John Maxwell: **leadership is influence.** You can see whether or not people have influence by whether or not anyone is following them. Look for the people others follow, and they will help you start where you are.

Who are the people you should be looking after? What habits, qualities, or attributes should they possess? Here are some key things I have found helpful:

TRUST YOUR FIRST IMPRESSIONS.

I can't train you on this or transfer how I know through a book, but I have a "superpower"—I had discernment before I got saved, and then after I became a Christian it seems God doubled down on the gift.

I lean on my gut impression of people. I struggle teaching others this, but I've found that great leaders all possess this ability to some degree. You must learn to trust your gut, your first impression.

Sometimes you will just see that spark in a person. It may come in the form of a strong handshake, an impressive first impression, or simply a gut feeling. Trust it when you do. Listen to their words carefully, and remember—don't chase after people!

LOOK FOR INITIATIVE.

Find the people who refuse to wait for permission to make something better. Anyone can bring up problems, but these people bring ideas to the table. Even if the ideas aren't amazing, at least they have some.

People with initiative create movement! A leader with initiative isn't just pointing out problems; they are working toward solutions.

LOOK FOR UNQUENCHABLE PASSION.

The best leaders have deep and immoveable resolve. You can teach skills, but you can't train passion.

People with resolve are often hard on themselves. They're demanding and a little stubborn. Why? Because they care! But they also have the energy to do what you have asked them to do.

You do need to determine if they are passionate about the vision. Do they share your values, like excellence, kindness, no gossip, and stewardship? Can they follow or do they want to lead? Do they want to accomplish what you want to accomplish?

LOOK FOR CHARACTER, NOT JUST COMPETENCE.

The only way to know if someone has character is to spend time with them, or talk to someone who has. Character outweighs competency. Always. This is the hardest thing to discern or ascertain. But think about what Scripture says: if someone doesn't have love, who cares what their skills are!

LOOK TO THEIR PAST.

The best indicator of future success is someone's past success. Did this person display leadership qualities and potential in the past?

Here are two question I ask to gauge a potential leader when we're hiring for a position:

What have you done?

This is a great hiring question because this isn't what was your previous job or what was your title or job description. This question is designed to find out something about the person.

In other words, "We know you've worked some places, and that you held down a job and got a paycheck. But have you done anything? Did you make anything better? Did you improve anything? Did you start anything?"

Knowing what you know about you, would you hire you?

Pause...and read the question again. Basically you are asking about their work habits and productivity and how much work they get done. You're asking about how they spend their discretionary time at work. How much time do they spend on the internet? How quickly do they change that web browser, when they're looking at things instead of working? How much time do they spend on their phones versus doing work?

WHAT ELSE SHOULD YOU LOOK FOR?

Look for people who show up on time and are never late. Those who repetitively show up late show a lack of self-discipline.

Look for those who are always ready to learn how things are done *regardless* of their dedication, experience, or maturity.

Look for people who are consistent in coming to church and show a dedication to it. Inconsistency may indicate a lack of maturity.

Be wary of those who tell you they were elders somewhere else, or who say who say they love this church in the same breath they bash their previous church.

Look for people who you enjoy being around. Why? Because you're going to be spending a lot of time around this person. They don't need to be someone just like you, but they do need to be someone you enjoy working with. Do they energize you or drain you?

Look for those who have a sense of self-awareness and present themselves well. (Bad body order may indicate a lack of self-awareness.)

You'll notice that I didn't list skills or competency, because those things can be taught. As we've explored in a previous chapter, culture is more important than skill or experience.

The old saying regarding selecting people is still true but I've expanded it here: look for Christians who are F.A.T.—faithful, available, teachable. Are they faithful with the little things? Are they available to give their time, talent, and tithe? And finally, are they teachable?

WHAT'S THE GREATEST ASSET TO LOOK FOR?

Remember teachability is the greatest success factor in selecting the right people. When people push back on basic tasks, those are red flags. They must be teachable.

Listen to the questions they ask, check their responsiveness to emails and text, and look for punctuality.

WHY IS TEACHABILITY SO IMPORTANT?

There was a study* done on leaders who were fast tracked, that analyzed why some leaders succeeded and others failed. Since usually only the best of the best are fast tracked, it might be surprising to learn that many failed. But the number one cause of derailment was poor people skills. These leaders didn't "play well in the sandbox." They were brilliant and had other great skills, but they had broken relationships.

The number two cause of derailment was an inability to adapt. These leaders didn't grow and change over time. They were inflexible people who don't like changes.

These are the people you don't want on your team!

---

* Larry Osborne, *Accidental Pharisees: Avoiding Pride, Exclusivity, and the Other Dangers of Overzealous Faith*

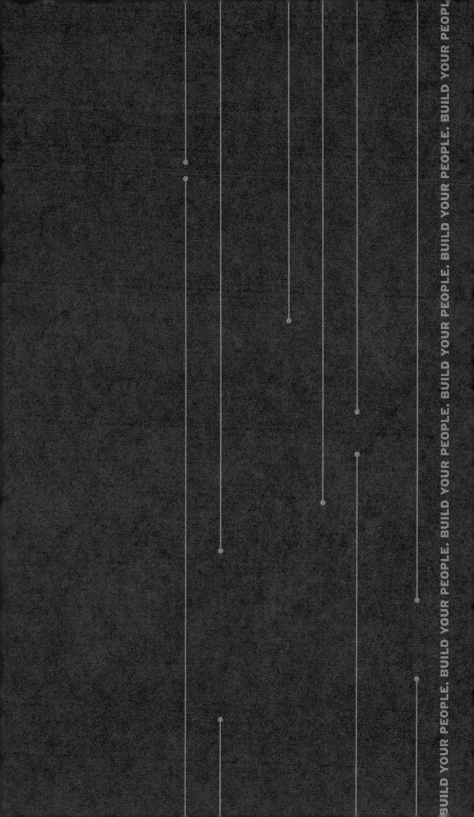

MINDSET SHIFT

Leaders are found one at a time. They don't respond to mass appeal, but through personal invitation and the sharing of a vision.

RECOMMENDED READING

○ *Exponential* by Dave Ferguson

○ *Hero Maker* by Dave Ferguson and Warren Bird

○ *Empowering Leadership* by Michael Fletcher

○ *How to Win Friends and Influence People* by Dale Carnegie

○ *Making Vision Stick* by Andy Stanley

Brush off Your Shoulder

It was the middle of February, and we were only five or six months old as a church plant. It was 7 a.m., and I drove our church truck to the location and began setting up. That morning we only had four people show up. What normally took 50 to 60 minutes took two and a half hours. We've all been in situations like this, when we're overwhelmed by the needs of the ministry.

The solutions we so often resort to rarely work. We communicate our need through mass appeal to our church by getting on stage, communicating the vision, and telling everyone what we need, and ask them to serve. We pass around a clipboard and say, "Please sign up!"

Usually twenty people sign up, and after the first meeting or assignment, five people stay. Within a few weeks, you discover that four out of the five aren't even the right kind of people you want on your team! Is there another way?

We need to remember leadership is about "followership." If you are leading but don't have followers, you aren't leading; you're holding a position. If a team is small and not growing, there is only one person responsible: the leader. Leaders must be team builders! The main job of every leader is to: identify, develop, and deploy other leaders.

Once you identified the right people as we discussed in the last chapter, what's next? What's the best way to recruit them?

Michael Fletcher at Manna Church in Fayetteville, North Carolina calls the next step "shoulder tapping." A shoulder tap is about using the power of a personal invitation and vision to recruit leaders to your team. It involves three steps: selection, connection, and vision.

SELECTION

We covered this in depth in the previous chapter, but the first step is to determine who are you looking for?

You're not looking for just any person. This isn't for everyone. Don't just look for people who breathe and speak English!

So often we select doers instead of leaders. What's the difference? Doers are people who do all the work. They do a good job, but they do it alone, and they ask based on need. They also don't involve other people. The ministry never grows under their leadership, or lack of it.

Leaders make things happen, while doers tend to respond to what's happening. Carey Nieuwhof writes, "Doers can take direction and execute someone else's vision, but they will require energy and follow-up that a leader doesn't require. A leader is a catalyst—creating change, momentum, and progress. You want to build your teams with people who make things happen."

If a leader is recruited, they will grow the ministry. They can't help it! Leaders will naturally build by recruiting other leaders.

Go after the best people, even if they are already on a different ministry team. Look for people who are already leading something even if it's not in the local church

Remember, the simplest definition of leadership is from John Maxwell: leadership is influence. You can see whether people have influence by whether or not anyone is following them.

CONNECTION

The next step is to personally approach this person and build a relationship. Get to know their name, and watch for patterns. Do they show up on time every week? Do they give consistency? If they have kids, are their diaper bags clean and orderly? These are all signs of a potential leader.

Yes, this is harder is larger churches, but the process is still the same. You will never know who your potential leaders are until you make a connection. So go make it happen!

VISION

An uninspired leader cannot inspire others. That's why the most important tool any leaders have is vision.

The idea here is to be a "vision based" recruiter by inviting others to be a part of something larger than themselves. Leaders want to be part of something they couldn't achieve on their own.

Doers respond to need but leaders respond to vision. So when making the actual ask, remember: raise the bar! Cast a big vision, and explain why it's important and why they may be the person for that role.

When I approach someone for a commitment, I'll often let them know I only have two to three slots available but will tell them I'm talking to five people. I'll remind them not everyone can do this role. Then I'll tell them not to give me an answer today, but to pray about it, seek what God has to say, and talk to their spouse before letting me know.

FURTHER WISDOM

Always pray and ask God to be at work when you make the ask. Be clear when you share with the person the vision of "why" and "what." Tell them why you believe they would be the ideal person to have in this role. And absolutely make the ask *clear!*

One thing I've found helpful when making the ask is to give a leader some statistic about the church. For example, "Did you know 80% of high school kids walk away from church in college? Let's change that in our church!"

Then I'll passionately cast the vision for why this can't happen without people rising up to meet the challenge. I call this an "upward draft" because it helps create a culture where others believe they can rise up too.

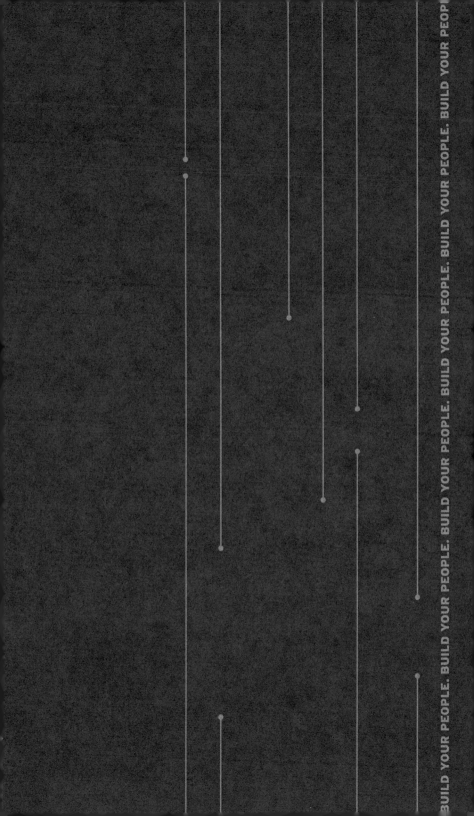

BUILD YOUR PEOPLE. BUILD YOUR PEOPLE. BUILD YOUR PEOPLE. BUILD YOUR PEOPLE. BUILD YOUR PEOPLE. BUILD YOUR PEOP

MINDSET SHIFT

You're not in the Sunday service business but in the people development business! Don't just build the church, build people.

RECOMMENDED READING

○ *Exponential* by Dave Ferguson
○ *The One Minute Manager* by Ken Blanchard
○ *Amplified Leadership* by Dan Reiland
○ *The 5 Levels of Leadership* by John Maxwell
○ *The Coaching Habit* by Michael Bungay Stanier
○ *Multipliers* by Liz Wiseman
○ *The Talent Code* by Daniel Coyle

11

How to Train Your Team

Here's a truth you need to embrace: you're not Jesus. You're probably thinking, "Thanks, Captain Obvious!" What I mean by that is that as strong as your leadership is and as much as God has given you the gift of discernment, at the end of the day you lack his omniscience and perfect wisdom when it comes to identifying and recruiting leaders.

You need a system to filter out your mistakes. As good as your gut instincts are about people, you can't foresee everything. This is the where the power of apprenticing comes in. It's the best way to build and train leaders. You're creating a system to develop people over a period of time, and the best will naturally rise to the top.

Why does apprenticing help with developing new leaders? Because here's a problem leaders typically experience: we give someone a big task only to have them drop it because they didn't do it correctly. Not only are you frustrated, but they are too! Who's to blame? You are! (If you disagree with me please go back and reread chapter one.) You need to grow as a leader. **Great leaders never blame. They always take responsibility.**

Failures happen because most leaders don't train other leaders properly! The mindset shift you need to embrace is that you need to reproduce your skills in another leader. You need to replace yourself, and that can only be done through proper training.

Don't just build the church, build the people in your church! They need to be trained! Why? Because doing doesn't reproduce. Leadership does. It takes great leadership and skill to move people from teams that do, to teams that lead. This is what proper training is all about.

WHAT IS APPRENTICING?

Apprenticing is about developing people. This is not discipleship. I think everyone should be discipled (as Jesus made clear) but not everyone should be developed as a leader. Be aware there's a difference between equipping (training for a skill) and developing (investing to make someone better).

Discipleship is about teaching spiritual things.

Apprenticeship is about equipping someone with skills.

In our church, we apprentice people by shoulder tapping them, as discussed in the previous chapter. We speak life and encouragement over these people as we see something God is doing in their lives. There is just something different about their faith and obedience to God that's obvious to others. We see potential and leadership, and we want to help them take the next step in their leadership.

WHY DO LEADERS NEED APPRENTICESHIP?

Frankly, if you don't have an apprentice, you're a poor leader. Most likely you are a great doer or a control freak, but either way you're a poor leader.

This process of discovering, training, and empowering other

people *grows* your leadership. Without this process, the ministry is built around you and is stagnant.

WHAT'S EXPECTED OF AN APPRENTICE?

Realize how you bring future leaders on board and how well you communicate with them is key to their success. They need to know what the next step is and to have clear expectations so they understand what's expected from them.

At CenterSet, every team has the same apprentice process. (It doesn't matter what team you are serving on, because leadership is transferable!)

We tell them for the next 8-10 weeks we will begin training them without a title. We have them sign a leadership covenant that talks about being faithful with their time, talent, and tithe. This leadership covenant is more powerful than a membership covenant because we are calling them to a different standard. Apprentices *must* live in obedience to Jesus.

In most churches, this standard is placed on anyone who serves.

We place this standard the moment you are being considered as a leader of others.

We then have every apprentice read two books: *It* by Craig Groeschel and *Empowering Leadership* by Michael Fletcher. These books explain the *why* and the *what* of our leadership approach.

We then spend the next 6-8 weeks teaching them our church's culture (see chapter six). During this process, every apprentice is appointed a team leader who they shadow for the next 8-10 weeks. Not only are they learning leadership, but the skills to lead a ministry area.

At the end of the apprenticeship, everyone is given a next step. Not everyone passes apprenticeship.

THINGS TO CONSIDER IN APPRENTICING PEOPLE

Busy people are sometimes better than available people. It's because they get things done. Be wise!

I recommend apprenticing two people at the same time, because this can product a healthy competition. One-on-one is sometimes a waste of time. You aren't creating an assistant, but training a leader, someone to replace you.

Never give a title without a timeline. For example, "Let's do this for X amount of weeks, and then we'll talk about the title." When someone knows they're being watched during training, they know they need to step their game up. At the same time, it's important to consider the fun factor and ask apprentices if they're having a good time and if this process is meeting their expectations.

WHAT'S THE BEST WAY TO TRAIN AND RELEASE APPRENTICES?

This process was first made famous by John Maxwell and then explained in *Exponential*.

I do. You watch. We talk.

Imagine I am leading the production team. The first time we meet, I tell my apprentice to simply come to observe me. I will lead the team, and all my apprentice will do is just watch and take notes. They will see how I interact, what I say, what I do, and how I lead the material. Then after the service is done, we chat about it.

I do. You help. We talk.

This time I involve my apprentice during the planning and preparation phase before the Sunday meeting. I'm still leading but now they are helping when I give them some small task. But they are still watching and learning, and again we chat afterwards.

You do. I help. We talk.

Getting to this phase may take one week or several months. It doesn't have to happen quickly—just don't skip a step.

You do. I watch. We talk.

This is the hardest step in the process because most leaders are control freaks. We feel we know better, faster ways of doing it. But Craig Groeschel once said that someone else doing a task at 65% of what you can do is still worth it!

You do. Someone else watches.

Your apprentice now has an apprentice! This is the ultimate sign you have reproduced yourself because they are doing in others what you did in them.

OTHER THINGS TO CONSIDER

The old adage is true: If you want to impress someone, bring them far; if you want to influence them, bring them close.

Be aware of how you handle critique during the apprentice process. We tend to be hardest on other people when we see in them the things we're hardest on ourselves about. Let your apprentices see you get critiqued. Why? This process builds a culture of healthy and positive correction.

Remember that what gets rewarded gets repeated. Structure and systems create behaviors and in the case of good systems, will actually increase freedom. (Think of a trampoline with a net. Knowing that net is there will encourage you to jump more boldly.) If you don't like the behavior or if something isn't working, first try changing the system. Always put people before process.

Learn to celebrate your apprentices' progress. Even small steps in the process are well worth acknowledging. Other people are watching and will watch how you encourage and inspire others.

TACKLING YOUR FEARS ABOUT APPRENTICESHIP

You may have some fears about apprenticing people, including asking them to do more than they are already doing. You may worry about training someone and then it doesn't work out. Some pastors may wonder, "If those on staff are being paid, should we be training others outside of the staff to do our job?"

I believe the answer to these fears is to remember this is about building people, not just doing the work that church requires.

DON'T FORGET YOU ARE AN APPRENTICE AND A LEARNER, TOO

You may feel that apprenticeship is for others, or something that you are only on the giving end of rather than the receiving end. But don't forget that everyone needs a mentor and ongoing training.

If Serena Williams, Tom Brady, and Michael Johnson need a coach, then you need one too. Please don't even argue about this! Go find someone to coach or mentor you.

How do you do this practically? Seek out someone from another church who is further along than you. For example, if you lead kids at a church of 200 people, go find someone at a church of 500. If you don't have a mentor, your time as a leader will end soon because you're not growing or being pushed.

I'm also a firm believer that leaders are readers. The moment you stop reading to grow as a leader, please step down from leadership. Don't just read a book—read it, take notes, and discuss it with someone. Why? Because you'll only retain 40% if you just read, but you'll retain 65% if you read and take notes, and 80% if you read, take notes, and discuss the content with others. I suggest getting together with a group, picking a book to read, and each time you gather, asking each other two good questions: "What are you learning?" and "How are you applying what you're learning?"

MENTORING VS. COACHING YOUR APPRENTICE

Leaders are not mass produced. They are instead made one on one. The goal is not just to delegate tasks but to delegate responsibilities. Michael Bungay Stanier states that coaching involves *"unlocking people's potential to maximize their own performance."* Coaching is an important and untapped aspect of leadership and development.

In coaching, asking questions helps people grow more than giving answers. Craig Groeschel* explains:

The best developers listen more than they speak. As leaders, we tend to want fast results. After all, we've got experience and wisdom, right? But people don't retain truth when you dump it on them, they retain it when they discover it for themselves. Ask questions that help people discover the answers. Lead into the question gently, and remove threats to the answer. Listen to their answers to understand their thought process instead of preparing your response.

Sometimes the best development for a leader doesn't come through mentoring, but coaching. This is why leadership development is an art, not a science.

One way to raise another leader is to allow him to observe you,

* https://open.life.church/training/315-craig-groeschel-leadership-podcast-how-to-develop-leaders

because they aren't just seeing your actions, but learning how you make decisions.

When you help your team to be more *self-sufficient*, you won't need to intervene all the time and become a bottleneck. It also frees you up to *focus on what truly matters* for you and your team. Coaching others pushes you and the people around you to step out of your comfort zones to *learn and grow*.

Here are the questions Michael Bungay Stanier shares in his book *The Coaching Habit*:

1. What's on your mind?
2. And what else?
3. What is the real challenge here for you?
4. What do you really want?
5. What do you want from me?
6. What could be being fully committed to the idea look like?
7. What was most useful for you?

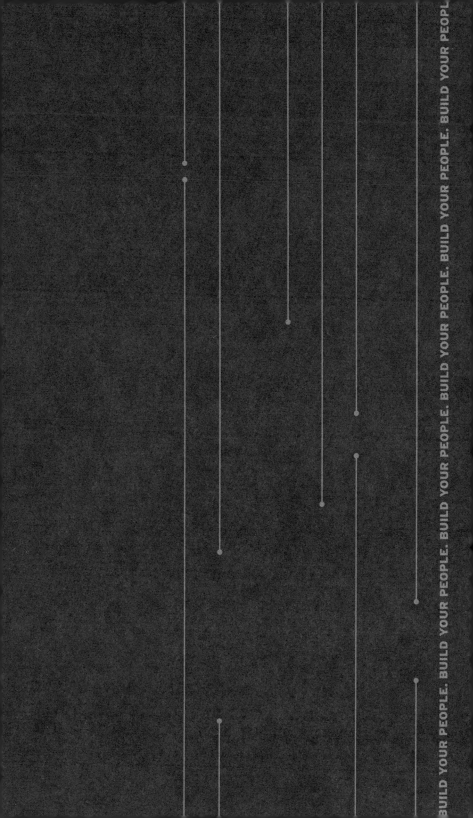

MINDSET SHIFT

If you don't clearly define leadership, others will define it for you.

RECOMMENDED READING

○ *One Minute Manager* by Ken Blanchard
○ *Leaders Made Here* by Mark Miller
○ *E Myth* by Michael E. Gerber

Delegate to Build

Most church leaders don't realize that preaching doesn't grow a church. Outreach and community service can draw a crowd, but also don't grow a church. It's leadership that grows churches.

For example, take a person with a level-10 leadership gift and a level-4 preaching gift and watch that church grow. However, if you reverse the gifting and take a level-10 communicator with a level-4 leadership gift, you'll find a very frustrated leader with a stagnant church. Why? Because leadership grows churches.

Too many leaders are multi-tasking instead of multi-leading. Multi-tasking is about you *doing* more. Multi-leading is about you *leading* more. When you train and delegate properly, you are not only releasing work that was once on your plate, but you are also focusing on developing that leader. As a church grows and the level of leadership needs to increase, this will require you to do less tasks but get more done.

How can you do that? By you doing less of the work and instead leading and coaching others to do those tasks. This is the difference between churches that grow and those that don't: great leaders develop others! Too many leaders keep adding to their plate as the size of their church increases, which is why most churches are below 100 people. This is the average number of people a single person who doesn't delegate can properly lead.

Most leaders think the more you give away, the less you're needed. However, the opposite is acutely true. The more you give away the greater job security you have, precisely because you are getting more done! Think about it: if you give a high capacity leader the ability to get 10 extra hours of work done per week without adding anything more to their plate, would they take it? That's exactly what proper delegating does.

If, for example, you work 50 hours, you can get 60 hours of work done with a high capacity volunteer to whom you've developed and delegated work to. This is why staff should be equippers, not doers, of ministry. Giving more away is powerful because if you lead this way, others below you will lead this way, and it will increase their capacity, too.

WHY DO SO FEW LEADERS DELEGATE?

One big reason why many leaders fail to delegate properly is they think if they hand off an important task to someone, that person will drop the ball completely. We get frustrated, lose trust, and blame others.

Most leaders falling into one of two extremes. We are either too hands on or too hands off. We either micromanage or abdicate completely. Neither approach works well, and causes leaders to think that delegating doesn't work.

Your ability to delegate says more about your humility than anything. Unfortunately, many leaders don't delegate because they are prideful and think they can do things better than those around them. While that might be true to some extent, we need to remember that ministry isn't about us. Jesus *always* works in teams. In fact, remember even Jesus delegated the money handling to others, which I'm sure he could have done himself. Why? Because delegation allow others to serve where they are called.

HOW DO YOU KNOW WHEN IT'S TIME TO DELEGATE?

In his book *E Myth*, Michael E. Gerber talks about how all small businesses are led by the owner. In the beginning, they do everything. For example, if someone had a bakery, the owner would arrive early to bake, sell the pastries and bread all day, and then stay late to clean up. But the business will never grow and change until the owner begins delegating and leading. Churches are the same way! In order to change, leaders must change how they think.

The process to arrive at delegation involves three phases: the technician phase, the manager phase, and the vision phase. Each phase requires your role and responsibility to change.

THE TECHNICIAN PHASE

In a church plant, the church planter and his wife are co-planting something together. It's a family affair. They are doing everything, from inviting, to designing, to social media posts, to calling people— literally everything. They are just like the bakery owners in the previous example!

The technician phase is categorized by survival, and you must do it or it won't get done because there is no one else. This phase is normal, but it's just that—a phase. If you're still in the same place after a few months or years, something is wrong.

THE MANAGER PHASE

In this phase, the owners hire people do tasks. For example, in the case of the bakery, they might hire a janitor to clean after a long day and cashiers to sell after they spend hours baking. They might even hire a good baker whom they trust with their recipes.

In this phase your role changes from doing to managing. Instead of you doing the actual work, you are delegating that role or responsibility to another.

Churches are the same way! But this step shouldn't just apply to paid staff; it should also apply to volunteer staff. You are looking for high capacity people who want to help build the local church.

THE VISION PHASE

This final phase is yet another level of delegation. In this phase, the bakery owner might open up another store. Since people can only be in one location at a time, they need to delegate the management of a store to someone else, and *that* person finds bakers, cashiers, and janitors! The idea is that you manage these managers, and they manage the stores. I'm sure you see the pattern here, but ideally churches should function in the same way!

HOW DO I DELEGATE EFFECTIVELY?

Delegation is less a formula and more a process, because it is more about trust and culture than skill and competency.

In his book *One Minute Manager*, Ken Blanchard puts meat and bones on this idea of delegation, which can apply to any business or church setting. He uses the terms Directing, Coaching, Supporting, and Delegating to describe the different phases of trust and responsibility until a role is fully delegated to someone. Many of our leadership issues are due to skipping these steps and still expecting exceptional results.

Please note that you should tell the person you are training about all four phrases before they begin. They should understand they are being trained for a role or ministry with the idea of it being delegated to them. (But remind them it will take time!)

DIRECTING

This is where the person you are training is told exactly what to do. For example, if they need to write an email, you give them the content, tell them who to send it to and when to send it, and then you ask them to do it. Another example of this would be asking someone to gather info about a subject. You might tell them to go find four or five movie theaters closest to a particular zip code.

In both cases, you're asking them to do something very specific. The results should always be the same so it's easy to measure if they did it well. You are evaluating them in this phase. How did they do their task? Were they late? Was their work clean? Did you like what they did? This is your opportunity to correct them now when the tasks and responsibly are small.

COACHING

In the coaching phase, you ask them to perform a task like write an email, similar to what you've done in the past. But before they send it, ask them to show it to you. In the previous phase, you gave them all the content and words. In this phase, you're testing if can they create it and repeat excellence.

Another idea is to ask them to research something, like the best software tool for a need your organization has. Ask them to not only research it but also to give their suggestions as to what they would choose. Again the goal is not to get the work done, but to teach them how to think and evaluate based on the culture and values of your organization.

SUPPORTING

In this phase, you're still coaching the person but you haven't fully released all responsibility. Instead, you're challenging them about whether there are better ways to get the job done.

I've been using sending emails as our example. To continue this example, in this phase, you don't tell them what to send or when to send it. But you might ask something like, "How many people are reading the emails we send out?" Or "Is Mail Chimp the best tool for this? What are other churches doing?" You're allowing them to research, learn, and decide what's best through you asking questions. But through this process, you're teaching them to think like you.

DELEGATING

In might surprise you, but in this phase, you check in on the person, not their task. Ask, "How's your marriage? How are your children?" Why do this? Because people who are healthy do great work.

At this phase, they have earned your trust and the respect of the organization to lead and direct their area. It takes time get there! I like to say that it takes time for a cucumber to become a pickle. Don't delegate too quickly or you might not get a pickle.

In their *Dream Team Coach's Playbook**, Journey Church provides these tips for empowering those you delegate to:

Give them the role. Once they have proven their character and ability, and you have adequately trained them, let them take the lead.

Give them space. Trust God and give them both opportunities to succeed and room to fail. Provide appropriate feedback for both. As you are handing things off, someone may do some things differently than you would. That is okay as long as the end result is still getting accomplished with excellence.

---

* https://open.life.church/training/315-craig-groeschel-leadership-podcast-how-to-develop-leaders

Give them time. It can take a year for someone to learn their new role.

Give them the benefit of the doubt. The leader will not get it right every time. They are learning and growing in leadership.

PRACTICAL TIPS FOR BETTER DELEGATION

Give yourself permission to give things away. Too many leaders feel bad for giving tasks and responsibilities to others. They shouldn't. Doing less means you are leading more! Remember you don't need to be the best at everything—you need to *find* the best and lead them.

Stop and re-evaluate your role to remind yourself of what you should and shouldn't be doing. This refocus helps you set priorities and clarify your tasks. It also helps shift your mindset and remove any task you shouldn't be doing

I recommend doing what I call a brain dump because great leaders don't store everything in their head. Sit down and figure out the fifty things you do each week, month, and quarter. Find a way to dump and plan and process it all. Think through which of those things you do better than anyone.

Remember that 85% of what you do can't be delegated because only you can do those things: brush your teeth, play with your kids, eat, sleep, etc. 10% of what you do could and should be done by someone else. The remaining 5% is the area you should focus on. They are the tasks that you can uniquely do.

After you do the brain dump, start thinking about *who* you can find and recruit to help you with those tasks. This step comes after you identify what you do that could be passed on to the right people.

However, remember this is about giving away *authority*, not just tasks. Don't give away a task, because it will come back to you. But if, through proper delegation, you give away leadership or authority over that area, the right person will own it, run it, manage it, and make it better. This is what you're after!

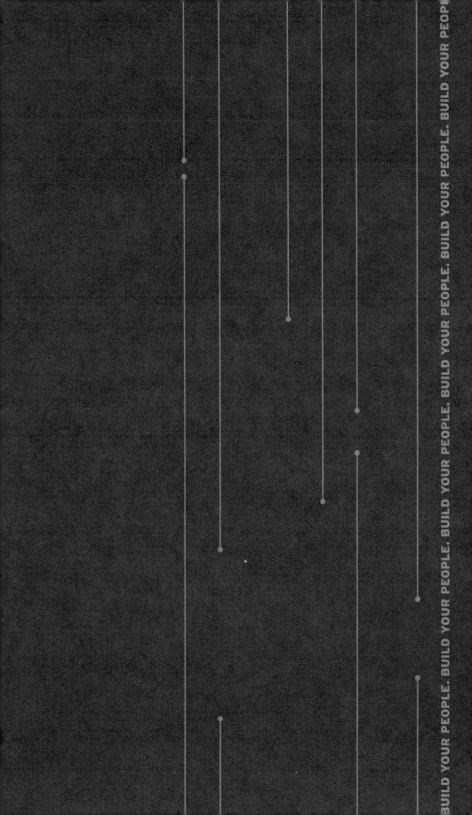

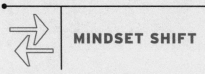

MINDSET SHIFT

The mission is more important than the position!

RECOMMENDED READING

- ○ *Multipliers* by Liz Wiseman
- ○ *Radical Candor* by Kim Scott
- ○ *The Ideal team Player* by Patrick Lencioni

How to Correct Your Team

What happens if you've followed all the tips and processes I've outlined in this book, but it's become clear someone isn't working?

I recommend beginning with questions. Never assume the worst in others! Find out what's going on first.

For example, in the early days of our church we would need to show up at 7 a.m. every Sunday for setup. Many times key leaders would show up late. They would walk in, avoid eye contact, and get to work. I would approach them calmly and gently say, "Is everything OK?" If they said, "Yes, everything fine," I would ask, "Did your car break down, or are you or your wife sick?" If they indicated no, I would ask, "Then why are you late?"

Remove extraneous circumstances and get to the heart of the issue. You don't know what's really going on inside of someone unless you ask! The issue is never just about job performance.

WHEN YOU'VE GOT THE WRONG PERSON ON YOUR TEAM

If that person is on your staff, blame HR and the hiring process. Find out who interviewed them, and what questions were asked.

If they are a volunteer, evaluate and check the process by which they were trained. Were they apprenticed correctly?

Many times we've found that we hired the wrong person for the wrong reasons. It's our leadership failure, not theirs. We should have been more diligent to discern and identify they were wrong for the role. This is why great organizations hire slowly, fire quickly.

THE RIGHT PERSON IN THE WRONG ROLE

When this happens, the person has the leadership, culture, and values that the organization emphasizes. However, the person is in a role that they are unable to succeed in. Sometimes that is OK! Simply move them to a role they can succeed in. This happens when personality and gifts tests aren't used to help identify where the person could best excel. It falls on the leader to discover, develop, and deploy their team member's God-given gifts and talents.

Craig Groeschel says,*

Self-awareness is the first step to growth and development. People have an unlimited capacity for self-deception. A problem someone doesn't know about is a problem they can't solve. People don't know what they don't know. The best foundation of future success is self-awareness in the present. As leaders, we can never assume people naturally become aware. Through tools, training, coaching, and testing, we can help create self-awareness.

...People must own their own development. Strive to give your team members two things: permission to fail and room to rise. They need permission to fail because

* https://open.life.church/training/315-craig-groeschel-leadership-podcast-how-to-develop-leaders

growth always involves the risk of failure. Push them out of their comfort zone. You aren't seeking perfection. You're seeking growth, and growth and comfort never co-exist. Remember, you don't have to know it all to be a great leader! Be yourself.

If you have leaders who are on board with your vision and values, but are in the wrong role, don't lose these people. Simply move them!

THE RIGHT PERSON IN THE WRONG CHURCH

Sometimes the leader in question really is a rock star. They have strong leadership skills, a great spirit, and are humble and hardworking, but you know they aren't the right person for the job because this isn't their church. Perhaps they have a theological disagreement that is so great it naturally creates tension.

Healthy and wise churches promote, recruit, and reward based on culture, not skill. In this scenario, you need to demote the person and let them go. You're actually holding them back from what God wants them to do!

HOW CAN YOU PREVENT HAVING THE WRONG PERSON?

Ultimately you can't always prevent this. Only Jesus knows all things and can foresee it all. But you can take steps to ensure you're doing your part. This includes having a strong and healthy hiring process, and a clear job description and measurable goals.

SO DO I JUST FIRE THEM?

No, not yet. Take each person through three phases to examine their performances issues. The final phase is graceful termination. I recommend recording everything through email so there is a paper trail.

You can also follow this same protocol with volunteers, only instead of firing them, you demote them and move them to another role.

Coaching

In this phase, you need to provide clear coaching for the individual. They need help to break through mindsets, behavioral patterns, or simply lack of experience—whatever is contributing to their poor job performance.

When you hire the right people, and you're part of a growing and thriving organization, everyone is being pushed. Those people should have coaches and should be learning from books. However, this isn't what I'm talking about here. This is specific coaching from their boss as to why they are not performing their specific job.

This phase needs to be clearly communicated. For example, "You're having job issues, and I would like move you to a coaching phase, because I believe in you and don't want to lose you. I think with proper coaching you can grow and overcome these issues."

People need to be told they are in this phase and that they are having performance issues. They need to understand why you are coaching them.

Growth plan with time cap

In this phase, coaching isn't cutting it. You need to light a fire under them and hope they don't get burned.

For example, perhaps someone is leading a kid's ministry or a worship ministry, and their job description clearly communicates they are called to identify, recruit, and train new leaders, only their team isn't growing. You could tell them they have 90 days to add three people to their ministry.

Growth plans are a set amount of time, with a specific and clear action goal. Each person in the conversation knows exactly what is expected. The boss is communicating, "If you don't do this, you're probably fired." The leader needs to be able to understand, "If I can do this, I stay in my role."

Don't forget to continue to provide coaching during this phase. People need encouragement and constant support so they know you believe in them. Jesus didn't quit on you, so don't quit on people.

Graceful termination

In this phase, you are releasing the person for a better role. This is best for you and them. Don't hold them back, and don't allow them to hold you back.

WISDOM FOR THIS PROCESS

I strongly believe in honoring the person throughout the whole process. People matter to God, whether or not they are good employees or volunteers. Remain in God's will and do it his way. Jesus is Jehovah Jireh. He will provide the leaders you need. Honor and trust him!

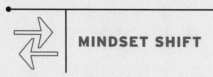

MINDSET SHIFT

Why is greater than what.

RECOMMENDED READING

○ *Start with Why* by Simon Sinek
○ *Making Vision Stick* by Andy Stanley

14

Inspire Your Team

"If you wish to build a ship, do not divide the men into teams and send them to the forest to cut wood. Instead, teach them to long for the vast and endless sea."

— *attributed to Antoine de Saint-Exupéry*

The authors of *The Flight of the Buffalo* (Warner Books, 1993) write, "Vision is the beginning point for leading the journey. Vision focuses. Vision inspires... Vision is our alarm clock in the morning, our caffeine in the evening. Vision touches the heart. It becomes the criterion against which all behavior is measured. Vision becomes the glasses that tightly focus all of our sights and actions on that which we want to be tomorrow—not what we were yesterday or what we are today. The focus on vision disciplines us to think strategically. The vision is the framework for leading the journey."

WHY IS VISION SO POWERFUL?

Vision moves people. It causes people to give, serve, and sacrifice because they see the big picture. Vision is the most powerful tool in a leader's pocket, because *it is a picture of the future that creates passion in people.*

Leaders who don't have vision can't motivate or inspire people. Proverbs talks about the power of vision to move people. Vision connects the why to the what. Need and vision both move people, but vision has staying power. Vision moves people to do things they would otherwise never do! A dream is about what God could do. A vision is about what God *will* do.

> "If people can't see what God is up to, they stumble all over themselves; but when they attend to what he reveals, they are most blessed."
> (*Proverbs 29:18, The Message*)

In the book *Talent Code*, the Windshield Effect is discussed. In 1997, there were no South Koreans golfers on the PGA tour. Today there are more than forty, and they win one third of all the tournaments. What happened? In 1998 Se Ri-Pak won a national golf tour. Million of South Korean girls were ignited by a new vision for themselves. They first saw it done by another, and they began to believe they could do it too! This is also why short people all across the country are now playing basketball. They saw Steph Curry shoot three-point shots and excel in a tall man's game. Now they're saying, "It could be me!" Your leaders need to have that experience with you.

EXAMPLES OF VISION

Henry Ford had a vision of every person in American owning a vehicle called the Model T. Martin Luther King Jr. had a picture of people of color coming together and no longer being judged by the color of their skin but by the content of their character. Steve Jobs had a vision for a computer for the rest of us, accessible and simple to use. Billy Graham had a vision for thousands of God's lost kids returning home and placing their faith in God's Son Jesus Christ.

For each of these people, their picture of the future made their hearts beat fast and their minds race. Their vision was their passion.

Let me share another example that shows the power of vision.

Imagine a person is walking down the street and sees a historic church in the process of restoration. As he passes by the construction site, he notices three different men building bricks and is curious to know what they are doing. Yet when this man asks the workers, he receives three different answers:

- The first construction worker says, "I'm building bricks."
- The second construction worker says, "I'm building a wall."
- The third construction worker says, "I'm building a church."

Which worker do you think had caught the vision?

In the same way, while good leaders get people to serve in their church, great leaders teach their people the *why* behind everything they do, based on the vision. This allows people to how they are connected to the bigger vision of church.

You might tell someone, "You aren't just holding a sign to greet guests. You're creating an environment of love for others to hear the gospel. You are the sermon before the sermon."

Or, if a servant leader is helping on the production team, we would tell them, "You aren't just pushing buttons on a computer, but removing distractions to allow people to get connected to God. You are removing the barriers of distractions so others can connect with Jesus!"

Or, "You aren't just setting up chairs and the stage. You are doing ordinary things so God can do extraordinary things. You are preparing environments for miracles."

Or, "You aren't just singing songs. You are creating environments where God is not merely studied but experienced."

WHY DOES VISION NEED TO BE REPEATED?

Simply put, vision leaks. People forget why they do things. Too often we focus on the what of what we do and not the why. This means good leaders cast vision one or two times and think things are fine. But great leaders cast the vision so often they feel like it's bleeding from their ears.

There is no science or proven research behind how often you should cast vision, but we do see a biblical example in the book of Nehemiah.

God gave a cup bearer named Nehemiah a vision to rebuild the walls of Jerusalem and restore God glory for God's people. Jerusalem's walls had been broken for 150 years, but Nehemiah didn't care. He had a God-given vision for restoration. This simple truth teaches us that vision is birthed in your prayer closet. It's a solo project. It begins with a dream in the heart of the leader, who sees what God wants to do in and through a group of people. Vision allows the leader to see beyond small numbers, financial difficulty, and impossibilities and see the future as if it is already here!

In the story of Nehemiah, vision was retold every 26 days. The *why* was re-communicated to instill faith, courage, resilience and perseverance. Leaders should take note—vision must be repeated constantly.

A leader begins a with dream and over time faith and confidence begin to grow and what the leader pictures can become a reality. Such a leader is living by more than just what they can see.

As the leader prays for God's vision, and wrestles with God about it, the vision often changes and grows, becoming bigger than something the leader could never have constructed himself.

HOW TO BUILD VISION INTO YOUR CHURCH

Because vision is about possibility, the work of a leader is to translate this possibility into reality.

Problem: The first step is to create tension by explaining a problem we all experience.

Solution: If the problem was stated properly, people will long for a solution.

Urgency: Vision should always create urgency for action now. People will think, "The problem will remain if we don't act!"

When we share the vision with others, it's not just about seeing potential in someone. It's about the ability to share the vision of the ministry and inspire people to action.

CORRECTIVE CONVERSATIONS AND VISION

Great leaders see problems as opportunities to show vision and culture. They don't get mad that people mess up, because it's not just about getting the job done but about growing people. Each problem is an opportunity to recast the vision of why we do what we do and why it's so important. People shouldn't feel guilty or shamed when they mess up, but instead understand the why behind everything we do. Vision is why, ministry is the what.

Remember: Don't just build the church, build its people!

How to Lead a Huddle

A huddle is when a team gathers together, usually in a tight circle, to strategize, motivate, or celebrate. Commonly the leader of the huddle is the team leader, and it is the leader who will try to inspire his fellow team members to achieve success. Similarly, after an event, a huddle may take place to congratulate one another for the team's success, or to commiserate a defeat.

WHY DO WE HUDDLE?

To strategize: In this case, we huddle to "call the play" for our team. If the church service flow requires an unusual play by our team, we figure out a strategy to go with.

To motivate: We use these huddles to remind our team of the value serving our guests so they can hear the message and make a decision for Christ.

To celebrate: These huddles allow us to celebrate the team and the number of salvations last week. Each number represents a heart given to Jesus!

A HUDDLE IS A TEAM ACTION

There is no "I" in team! As a team, we love to develop relationships, pray for each other's individual needs, and help each other take next steps.

But, we don't do that in the huddle—we do that in our fellowship time before and after our serve and in communication between when we're serving. The huddle is for the team as a unit.

Sharing prayer requests and individual needs in the huddle takes our hearts and minds to ourselves, when our focus should be on those we're serving. We're there to serve them, not ourselves.

TIME COUNTS

Just as time counts in a game huddle, time is important in our team huddles. Huddles should only be five to seven minutes long. We call the play, motivate the team, celebrate what we get to do, and pray the team out!

THE "WINS" OF AN EFFECTIVE HUDDLE

Huddles are the only "team meetings" we have with Dream Team members, except for Team night. (At CenterSet, we call each of our leadership/volunteer groups Dream Teams.) The Dream Team Culture remains strong and clear when our leaders offer effective huddles.

When we do huddles, we get clarity of why we get to serve today and what the serve should look like. There is full team awareness of changes that will affect our service. Everyone is "in the know," so we're communicating that everyone matters! These huddles are all about team, less about me. They provide an important opportunity to celebrate what we get to be a part of...someone's salvation story!

The Power of Checklists

MINDSET SHIFT

If you don't clearly define leadership, others will define it for you.

RECOMMENDED READING

○ *The Checklist Manifesto: How to Get Things Right* by Atul Gawande

WHAT IS A CHECK LIST?

It is a list of tasks that need to be performed. Each job would in essence have a different checklist.

In the book *Checklist Manifesto*, I learned that when doctors and nurses in the ICU create their own checklists for what they think should be done each day, the consistency of care improves to the point where the average length of patient stay in intensive care dropped by half.

WHY USE A CHECKLIST?

It allow you to better delegate responsibility without having to re-peat yourself, thus ensuring quality and consistency stay the same!

BENEFITS OF CHECKLISTS

- Checklists protect us against failure.
- Checklists establish a higher standard of baseline performance.
- Checklists allow others to be trained faster because oral train-ing is reduced.
- In the end, a checklist is only an aid. If it doesn't aid, it's not helping you.

THOUGHTS FROM CHECKLIST MANIFESTO

- "The volume and complexity of what we know has exceeded our individual ability to deliver its benefits correctly, safely, or reliably. Knowledge has both saved us and burdened us."
- "Whether running to the store to buy ingredients for a cake, preparing an airplane for takeoff, or evaluating a sick person in the hospital, if you miss just one key thing, you might as well not have made the effort at all."
- "A further difficulty, just as insidious, is that people can lull themselves into skipping steps even when they remember them.
- "Checklists seem to provide protection against such failures. They remind us of the minimum necessary steps and make them explicit. They not only offer the possibility of verification but also instill a kind of discipline of higher performance."
- "Checklists seem able to defend anyone, even the experienced, against failure in many more tasks than we realized."
- "Three different kinds of problems in the world: the simple, the complicated, and the complex."